Anton Piatigorsky

Two Plays

The Offering

The Kabbalistic Psychoanalysis
of Adam R. Tzaddik

The Offering

&

The Kabbalistic Psychoanalysis of Adam R. Tzaddik

by
Anton Piatigorsky

Playwrights Canada Press
Toronto • Canada

Playwrights Canada Press
54 Wolseley Street, 2nd Floor
Toronto, Ontario CANADA M5T 1A5
416-703-0201   fax 416-703-0059
info@puc.ca   http://www.puc.ca

Playwrights Canada Press acknowledges the support of
The Canada Council for the Arts for our publishing programme and
the Ontario Arts Council.

Production Manager: Jodi Armstrong

National Library of Canada Cataloguing in Publication Data

Piatigorsky, Anton, 1972-
    Two plays

Contents: The kabbalistic psychoanalysis of Adam R. Tzaddik – The
offering.

ISBN 0-88754-624-2

    I. Title. II. Title: The kabbalistic psychoanalysis of Adam R.
Tzaddik. III. Title: The offering.

PS8581.I218T96 2001   C812'.6   C2001-902338-3
PR9199.4.P479T96 2001

First edition: October 2001.
Printed and bound by AGMV Marquis at Quebec, Canada.

For my father,

Joram Piatigorsky

ACKNOWLEDGEMENTS

Chris Abraham's excellent dramaturgy greatly helped develop both plays.

Thanks to the actors and outside voices who influenced these plays in workshops and productions: Dean Gilmore, Graeme Somerville, Terrence Bryant, Paul Fauteux, Gary Reineke, Liisa Repo-Martell and Mark Ellis.

I have profited, thankfully, from many books. For my play *The Kabbalistic Psychoanalysis of Adam R. Tzaddik*: *The Introductory Lectures on Psychoanalysis, Three Essays on the Theory of Sexuality, Therapy and Technique*, and *The Interpretation of Dreams* by Sigmund Freud; *Major Trends in Jewish Mysticism, On the Mystical Shape of the Godhead*, and *On the Kabbalah and its Symbolism* by Gershom Scholem; *The Zohar*, translated and edited by Daniel C. Matt; *The Essential Kabbalah* by Daniel C. Matt; *The Mystic Quest* by David S. Ariel; *Meditation and Kabbalah* by Aryeh Kaplan; *Sigmund Freud and the Jewish Mystical Tradition* by David Bakan; *Circle in the Square* by Elliot R. Wolfson. For my play *The Offering*: *Difficult Freedom, Time and the Other, Totality and Infinity*, and *Otherwise Than Being or Beyond Essence* by Emmanuel Levinas; *The Levinas Reader*, edited by Seán Hand; *Adieu to Emmanuel Levinas*, and *Writing and Difference* by Jacques Derrida; *The Akedah* by Louis A. Berman, as well as the more obvious influences.

I would especially like to thank Professor Elliot R. Wolfson for his terrific lectures on Jewish Mysticism at New York University. I would also like to thank Dr. Stephen Kwass, my parents, Auran, Ava and Sivan.

TABLE OF CONTENTS

THE OFFERING

The Offering was first produced by Moriah Productions in association with Ashkenaz at Artword Theatre, Toronto, from March 19-April 9, 2000, with the following cast and crew:

Abraham/Isaac/Jacob   Gary Reineke
Isaac/Jacob/Joseph   Mark Ellis
The Ram/Esau/Farrow   Dean Gilmour

Directed by Chris Abraham
Assistant Directed by Liisa Repo-Martell
Stage Managed by Stephen Souter
Production Managed by Chris Prideaux
Set and Costumes Designed by James Cameron
Lighting Designed by Rebecca Picherack
Composer/Musician: Ben Grossman

CHARACTERS

ACT I   ABRAHAM
              ISAAC
              THE RAM

ACT II   ISAAC
              JACOB
              ESAU

ACT III   JACOB
              JOSEPH
              FARROW

ACT ONE

> *A mountain top, open vista. There are stones, sticks and garbage scattered over the site. ISAAC sits on a rock, smoking quietly. ABRAHAM stands apart, holding a hiking bag, looking out at the view.*

ABRAHAM Isaac! *(pause)* Isaac, come here! Look at this! Over here!

ISAAC I can see from here, Dad.

ABRAHAM But it's better... I mean...

ISAAC What?

ABRAHAM Standing here. Where I stand. It's really... you have to...

> *Pause. ABRAHAM looks at him.*

We made it.

ISAAC Uh-huh.

ABRAHAM Didn't we?

ISAAC Yeah.

ABRAHAM I thought we couldn't quite do it, there, for a while. *(pause)* Beautiful walk, though. *(pause)* Tough. I'm not exactly a young man anymore. Not strong, like I used to be. Like you.

> *Pause. He looks at the view.*

Amazing. All for something, isn't it? All has its big pay off. *(pause)* Doesn't it?

ISAAC Sure, it does.

ABRAHAM You can give the view a good look from over there?

ISAAC	Mm-hm.
ABRAHAM	Isaac?
ISAAC	Yeah?

Long pause. ABRAHAM puts down his bag. He sits next to ISAAC. ISAAC smiles at him, weakly, and continues to smoke.

ABRAHAM You feeling alright? *(pause)* I mean, nothing's wrong?

ISAAC I feel fine, Dad.

Pause. ABRAHAM opens his bag and starts to unload it. He removes a number of items, including a large hunting knife wrapped in a worn oil-skin. ISAAC watches.

ABRAHAM Places like this are amazing to me. They make me feel so small. There's too much around me. I feel, somehow, I should take it all in. It's frightening, really.

ABRAHAM unwraps the knife and carefully places it on the ground. ISAAC stares at the knife.

Can you imagine being trapped up here in a storm? Held hostage in this barren place. Alone, in a tent, shivering and naked and stuck inside skin.

He laughs.

Imagine that! *(pause)* Hello?

ISAAC Yeah?

Pause. ABRAHAM smiles, then looks out.

ABRAHAM Oh, Isaac, look! Such astounding beauty. So bright! Such overwhelming scope, this light! Feels like I'm going blind, from exposure. You understand what I mean?

ISAAC	You're not going blind.
ABRAHAM	How do you know?
ISAAC	Well, you just said you saw the view.

ABRAHAM laughs.

ABRAHAM	That's very good.
ISAAC	Thanks.
ABRAHAM	You're very funny.
ISAAC	I am?

Pause.

ABRAHAM	Maybe we should build a fire.
ISAAC	Alright.
ABRAHAM	Maybe gather some wood.

ISAAC stands. He starts to gather scattered sticks into a pile. ABRAHAM watches for a moment. He stands and starts to help ISAAC.

ABRAHAM	I've been... I'm having trouble sleeping. *(pause)* I... uh... I don't really know what to do...
ISAAC	Trouble sleeping?
ABRAHAM	Yes.
ISAAC	Maybe you should take something.

ISAAC continues to pick up sticks.

ABRAHAM	Uh... well... I could, I suppose, but...
ISAAC	But what?
ABRAHAM	I don't really think that's the problem.

ISAAC   It isn't?

ABRAHAM   No. I'm thinking a lot about you. *(pause)* I'm think-
               ing about how to speak to you.

ISAAC   You don't have to think about that. Just talk, Dad.

ABRAHAM   I know, I... I mean, I'm trying. *(pause)* It's only...
               sometimes I think, when I'm trying, and it's not
               working, I think: How can I do it?

ISAAC   Just say what you have to say.

ABRAHAM   That's not really it.

ISAAC   Well, I don't know, Dad.

ABRAHAM   It's more, when I'm talking to you, or trying,
               rather, I think: it's not really important what I'm
               saying. It's only important that you hear me. That
               the words are heard. That they reach you instead
               of just drifting off this mountain top and falling
               down below. *(pause)* What I mean is... if you don't
               hear me... if I'm just standing alone and talking....
               (pause) Hello?

ISAAC   I'm listening, Dad.

ABRAHAM   You are?

ISAAC   Of course.

ABRAHAM   You understand me?

ISAAC   Sure, Dad.

               Pause.

ABRAHAM   Are you annoyed with me for saying this?

ISAAC   No.

ABRAHAM   Oh. Good.

ISAAC continues to gather sticks. ABRAHAM watches him for a moment. He wanders forward and looks at the view.

This place. *(pause)* I wonder if I could buy...

ISAAC stops working. He looks at ABRAHAM.

I don't see why not. It only takes money, and Lord knows, I've got enough of that!

He chuckles.

Maybe build a house up here. With this view. *(pause)* You'd come visit, wouldn't you?

ISAAC   It's a national park, Dad.

ABRAHAM   Well, some place just like it. You'd come visit?

ISAAC   I don't see why not.

ABRAHAM   I'll do it. A huge mansion on a mountain top.

ABRAHAM looks at the view.

So many years sequestered in my office, buying and selling, accumulating millions, and for what? For us, Isaac. So I can build my home in face of a terrifying view. *(pause)* You could come visit with your children.

ISAAC   I don't have children, Dad.

ABRAHAM   Not yet, no. *(pause)* You'd always be welcome. You'd never have to ask.

ISAAC   Thanks. *(pause)* Are you alright, Dad?

ABRAHAM   No.

Pause.

ISAAC   I'm going to get back to work, now. The sun's going to set pretty soon.

> *ISAAC starts to gather sticks again. ABRAHAM watches him.*

ABRAHAM   Start gathering stones. I think we have enough wood.

ISAAC   Stones?

ABRAHAM   Yes.

ISAAC   Alright.

> *ISAAC picks up a large stone.*

ABRAHAM   You're such a mystery to me.

> *ISAAC stops and looks at ABRAHAM.*

I can't... sometimes... I can't even think.... *(pause)* What was I saying?

> *Pause.*

ISAAC   Dad, are you alright? Are you sick?

ABRAHAM   What?

ISAAC   I mean, have you been checked? Your memory?

ABRAHAM   I remember everything.

ISAAC   Oh. Good.

ABRAHAM   I remember the moss green booties you wore on your first day back from the hospital. After you were born. Your first full day in the world.
I remember the small, white, bell-shaped, alpine flowers. We passed them by the thousands, on the way up. In the last two hundred meters before we reached the summit.

ISAAC   They were beautiful flowers.

ABRAHAM   Yes.

ISAAC   Looked like snow.

ABRAHAM   That's right. They did.

ISAAC   I'm glad you remember that, Dad.

ABRAHAM   Yes. *(pause)* I'm so alone.

              ISAAC shifts.

              What?

ISAAC   I need to put the stone down, Dad.

ABRAHAM   Put it by the wood.

              ISAAC puts the stone down.

              Are you listening to me?

ISAAC   Yeah.

ABRAHAM   So?

ISAAC   So... what?

ABRAHAM   So, I'd like to know... I mean, you're my son.

ISAAC   Yeah.

ABRAHAM   Well, you're a musician. What do you do all day?

ISAAC   I play music.

ABRAHAM   That's it?

ISAAC   And write music.

ABRAHAM   Do you like that?

ISAAC   Sure.

ABRAHAM   A lot?

ISAAC	I love it.
ABRAHAM	What does that mean? For you to love it?
ISAAC	Same as for everyone, Dad.
ABRAHAM	But... what do you feel?
ISAAC	Dad...
ABRAHAM	Tell me! *(pause)* Isaac, please.
ISAAC	I don't know.
ABRAHAM	Try.
ISAAC	I.... It makes me feel... happy.
ABRAHAM	That's not very specific.
ISAAC	It's music, Dad. I just play.

ISAAC has removed and lit another cigarette.

ABRAHAM	There's more.
ISAAC	There is?
ABRAHAM	Open up and say more!
ISAAC	I... I'm sorry.

Pause.

ABRAHAM	No. It's me. I haven't really slept in six weeks.
ISAAC	You should definitely get some pills.

ISAAC starts to pick up another stone.

ABRAHAM	I keep having this dream. It reoccurs. I'm sitting with my father in the desert and I won't speak. My father asks me questions but I don't answer them. Maybe I've no tongue, or haven't learned

how to use it. Maybe I'm just being stubborn. Hours pass. The emptiness is unbearable. We are sitting, silent, in the desert. Finally, my father pulls a knife, this knife, and hands it to me. He says: 'If you won't speak to me, then cut your words into the sand. The words will blow away, but not before I read them.' So I take the knife. Cut my words into the sand. And where I cut, the sand begins to bleed. Blood in the shape of letters. When I finish the cutting, I look at my father. But now my father... he's bleeding from the mouth. I'm upset. Then I realize: there's blood in my mouth, too. I try to spit it out, but when I do, words start dripping from my lips. Blood words. The words I've written in the sand. I'm speaking them. I'm astonished.

>   *Pause.*

ISAAC   That's your father's knife?

ABRAHAM   Yes.

ISAAC   I was wondering. Can I see it?

ABRAHAM   No. *(pause)* He gave it to me. *(pause)* I wouldn't want you to get hurt.

ISAAC   I won't get hurt.

ABRAHAM   It's sharp. It cuts and bleeds more than sand!

ISAAC   I'm a grown man, Dad. I'll be careful.

>   *Pause.*

ABRAHAM   My dream, I was saying–

ISAAC   You know, we have to set up camp. The sun's almost down.

ABRAHAM   Oh.

ISAAC   Do we have enough stones?

ABRAHAM	I think so, yes.
ISAAC	I'll build the fire. You put up the tent.

> *ISAAC starts to build a fire. ABRAHAM watches him.*

ABRAHAM	Isaac, can I ask you... I want to ask...?
ISAAC	What?
ABRAHAM	Do you ever feel so... I mean, so...
ISAAC	Just say it, Dad.
ABRAHAM	Weighed down and burdened by life.
ISAAC	What are you talking about?
ABRAHAM	As though life were asking me a question. And I'm responsible for the answer. I don't have an answer in me. I can only look at you. You, over there. *(pause)* There's no way to relieve my burden. I can only look at you and plead. *(pause)* Do you ever feel that?
ISAAC	I... I don't think I know what you mean...
ABRAHAM	It's so simple! *(pause)* Isaac, talk to me! You owe me!
ISAAC	I do?
ABRAHAM	You're my son! *(pause)* Speak! Now!
ISAAC	I can't, Dad. I... I can't...
ABRAHAM	You didn't answer my question!
ISAAC	Dad... the sun's going down. *(pause)* What are the stones for?
ABRAHAM	To put under the meat when I cut it.

ISAAC What meat?

ABRAHAM I brought some dried meat.

ISAAC Oh.

> *ISAAC continues building the fire. ABRAHAM grabs several sticks. Holding his knife, he is about to start cutting stakes for the tent. ISAAC looks up at him. ABRAHAM holds up the knife and a stake.*

ABRAHAM Stakes. For the tent.

> *ISAAC nods. ABRAHAM watches ISAAC work on the fire. He still holds the knife.*

Thank you for coming with me. On this trip.

ISAAC It's alright.

ABRAHAM I don't get to see you very often.

ISAAC No.

ABRAHAM Not as much as I'd like.

ISAAC Work.

ABRAHAM Yes.

ISAAC Keeps you busy.

ABRAHAM Always. *(pause)* It's going great, though. Business is booming. All coming together, at last. I feel in full command.

ISAAC Making lots of money.

ABRAHAM Tons.

ISAAC Mm-hm.

ABRAHAM In fact, I'm going to retire at the end of the year. And probably give you a big gift. The kind of gift you can live off for the rest of your life.

ISAAC   Oh. *(pause)* Wow.

ABRAHAM   All my wealth, like a throne.

ISAAC   Thank you.

               Pause.

ABRAHAM   It's my life-long ambition. It's everything I've
               always wanted. It's so that you and your children
               and their children and then their children can live
               totally free, unburdened and bountiful lives. So
               you don't ever have to worry.

ISAAC   Are you mad at me?

ABRAHAM   What?

ISAAC   Are you... I don't know...

ABRAHAM   No.

               Pause.

ISAAC   Thank you, Dad. That's a wonderful offer.

ABRAHAM   It's a horrible burden.

ISAAC   It is?

ABRAHAM   You'll be in constant debt. A life-long comfort that
               you'll always owe to me. A debt you can never
               repay. *(pause)* But you'll take it, Isaac! It's yours!
               I've willed it!

ISAAC   Okay.

               Pause.

ABRAHAM   Okay? *(pause)* Say something, god damnit! Are you
               even here? Say something to me!

ISAAC   Maybe I should go.

        ISAAC stands.

ABRAHAM   No. Wait.

        ISAAC picks up his bag.

ISAAC   You're scaring me, Dad.

ABRAHAM   Don't go. I won't scare you. Just stay. I want you to stay. *(pause)* Tell me what you're thinking. *(pause)* You have got to speak. *(pause)* Maybe if I tell you.... *(pause)* Isaac, I... I'm in trouble... I feel the world all around me. It's an oppressive weight pushing me from every direction. I can look around, take it all in, but it doesn't have any meaning for me. I'm left blind, without an answer. Except for you. I see you standing there, my answer, but you seem so far away. And speaking to you... this, it's... useless. The words come out, but they just circle around in the air until they're sucked back into me. I'm like a big black hole. I'm trying to meet you, Isaac. Face to face. So what can I do? When these words can't seem to bridge...? *(pause)* You and I, we have the same blood. We both are the same. Why are you so foreign? You know, I'd give up my life for you. You don't even have to ask, I've already offered it, completely. Could you do the same? Could you give me your life, as a gift, as a bridge? For me? An answer, a paying of debts? *(pause)* You don't understand. I'm talking and it's nothing but noise. *(pause)* Nothing. A cruel joke. *(pause)* Maybe that would be better. If we said nothing else of importance. If I had a son who'd only make jokes.

        Pause.

ISAAC   I don't know any jokes, Dad.

        Pause.

ABRAHAM   Is that supposed to be a joke?

        ISAAC shakes his head.

ABRAHAM   I don't think I have anything more to say to you.

> *ABRAHAM looks at the view, holding the knife.*
> *Pause. ISAAC puts down his bag. He takes out*
> *another cigarette and lights it. He goes to look out*
> *at the view with his father.*

ISAAC   Pretty bright, huh? Sun's gonna set, soon. *(pause)*
Should be nice from up here.

> *ABRAHAM nods. ISAAC coughs.*

Smokes. They'll kill you, these things. I've been
meaning to quit. Some say, the only way to quit is
cold turkey. But I don't know. I prefer the gradual
withdrawal.

> *ISAAC smokes.*

Hey, Dad, you want a drink?

> *ABRAHAM looks at ISAAC. Pause.*

I've got wine. We can share it.

> *ISAAC stomps out his cigarette. He goes to his bag*
> *and removes a bottle of wine. He opens it.*

It's cheap. I should've thought ahead. Brought a
nice bottle.

> *ISAAC holds out the bottle for ABRAHAM.*
> *ABRAHAM doesn't take it. Pause. ISAAC drinks.*

Yuck. Pretty crappy.

> *ISAAC smiles. He takes another drink, then stares*
> *out at the view.*

Look at that. Amazing, isn't it? Away it goes, the
sun.

> *There is a noise behind them. THE RAM enters.*
> *He wears an open shirt. He has on fluffy pants,*

> *like goat legs, a backpack, and a hat with horns on it. Still, he looks and acts like a hiker on a day trip.*

THE RAM   Whooo-eee!

> *THE RAM staggers, dizzily.*

God, my head is all – bbblllllppphhhhh – you know! Practically sprinted up those last two hundred feet!

> *THE RAM blinks his eyes. He sees ISAAC's wine.*

Lordy-lord! I think I need a refreshment. Whadda ya got, there, sport?

> *ISAAC hands him the bottle of wine.*

ISAAC   Here.

THE RAM   Well, hell-o vin-o!

> *THE RAM takes a drink.*

Mama-mia!

> *THE RAM looks out over the vista.*

Hot damn!

> *He points.*

You see that? Now that is a sunset! I can't believe I made it!

> *THE RAM laughs. He goes to ISAAC.*

I'm Ram. *(pause)* The name's Ram.

ISAAC   Isaac.

THE RAM   Hello, hello, hello!

ISAAC laughs.

Thanks for the wine.

ISAAC   It's alright.

THE RAM goes to ABRAHAM.

THE RAM   Hey, there, pops! I'm Ram! Nice to meet you!

He shakes ABRAHAM's hand.

ABRAHAM   Hello.

THE RAM sees ABRAHAM's knife.

THE RAM   Hey, nice knife. Can I see it? *(pause)* Come on! I'm a natural outdoors man!

THE RAM laughs.

So how about it? *(pause)* If I make you laugh, will you give it to me?

Pause.

ABRAHAM   Alright.

THE RAM   Great! *(pause)* So what's a buxom guy like you, doing in a barren place like this? *(pause)* Hello? You gotta problem or something? You look a little pale, you know. Kind-a sickly.

ABRAHAM   I'm not feeling very well.

THE RAM   Let me guess... you got, what, diarrhea?

ABRAHAM   No.

THE RAM   Scabies?

ABRAHAM   No.

THE RAM   Schistosomiasis?

Pause. ABRAHAM smiles.

THE RAM   You laughed!

ABRAHAM   That's a smile, not a laugh.

THE RAM   Oh, you want to get fancy-pants with the terms, do ya? *(pause)* So seriously. What's your problem?

ABRAHAM   I'm depressed.

THE RAM   No! Really? Well, it's yer lucky day! Rammy-boy's here to cheer you up!

> *THE RAM whips out a pan flute and starts to play a few notes. ABRAHAM stares.*

THE RAM   Hey, you like the flute or what?

ABRAHAM   Why not.

> *THE RAM plays a few bars, a lively pastoral tune. He plays a pitch, then tests his voice.*

THE RAM   Me-me-me-me.

> *He clears his throat, then sings, very fast:*

There once was a man named Abraham
Who smelled like a donkey's ass
This Abraham, he had a mule
That he named Sassafras, his lass.

Now, Sassafras, smelly Abraham's ass,
Lived in a field of grass.
And upon this ass named Sassafras
Sat Abraham, on his ass, in the grass
Oh, Sassafras was a very sad ass
When Abraham's ass passed his grass
'Cause Abraham's ass smelled of gas,
Poor Sassafras, Abraham's ass-lass.

> *THE RAM laughs. ISAAC and ABRAHAM smile.*

I'm just teasing.

ABRAHAM   Yes.

THE RAM   So, you laughed?

ABRAHAM   Not even close.

THE RAM   Well, I didn't mean to cheer you up with that!
                Pppfff!

> *He dumps the pan flute.*

Little rhymie-dimey song! Antiquated pan-flute!
Dancing around like some stupid goat-boy in
fluffy pants! Ha!

ABRAHAM   It's all Greek to me!

> *THE RAM laughs.*

THE RAM   Hey, that's funny! You're a funny guy! Okay, I got
                the thing. You, Isaac, punch me in the arm!

ISAAC   What?

THE RAM   Come on! I can take it! Punch me!

> *ISAAC punches him.*

THE RAM   Ow!

> *THE RAM punches him back, hard.*

ISAAC   Hey!

THE RAM   Not so god damn hard!

ABRAHAM   Don't punch him.

THE RAM   Oh yeah?

> *THE RAM gets in ABRAHAM's face.*

What're you gonna do about it, tough guy?

> *They stare at each other. Awkward pause. THE RAM starts to laugh, then pats ABRAHAM on the back.*

A lot of times people laugh when they get nervous.

ABRAHAM   Right.

> *THE RAM stares at the sun set, truly awed.*

THE RAM   Look at that sun! Not much time in it, huh?

> *Pirate voice.*

Thar' she goes! Aarrrrrrrrr! Walkin' tha' great big plank 'n the sky!

> *THE RAM nods, seriously.*

So you guys are just, uh, watching the sunset, then?

ISAAC   Yeah.

THE RAM   Nice, nice. You two know each other?

ISAAC   He's my father. I'm his son.

THE RAM   Greeaat! Father-son. Good to see in this day and age. Little bonding. Little climb the mountain, watch the sun. Oh, that's nice. My father's got a bit of a halitosis problem so I try not to spend too much time with him, if you know what I mean.

> *THE RAM fans his face, as if fanning away bad breath. ISAAC laughs.*

But it's great when it works, just great. *(THE RAM looks at ABRAHAM.)* Well?

> *ABRAHAM smiles and shakes his head.*

It's alright. I'm just getting started.

ABRAHAM   Forget it. It's no use.

THE RAM   Come on! I can do it!

ABRAHAM   If you don't mind, I'd like to be alone now. With my son.

THE RAM   Oh yeah? Alone? Why?

ABRAHAM   That's not your business.

THE RAM   Not my business? Am I not sharing this mountain top with you? Am I not your pal? You can tell me!

ABRAHAM   Look... I'm trying–

THE RAM   Trying what? *(to ISAAC)* He's trying something?

ISAAC   Uh... well...

THE RAM   Ohhhh. Father-son chit-chat. I get it. Serious time. Glad I came and saved you, eh, champ?

> *THE RAM pokes ISAAC with his elbow, and laughs. ISAAC smiles.*

Hey, so how long 'til it actually, you know?

> *ABRAHAM is staring at ISAAC.*

Hey, pops! When's the old turd in the sky gonna plop!

> *ISAAC laughs. ABRAHAM looks at his watch.*

ABRAHAM   Three minutes, fifty-two seconds.

THE RAM   Three minutes fifty two seconds! Lord almighty, where's the television up here, huh?

> *THE RAM laughs.*

That's, like, eternity! Three fifty-two! Damn! You're like a stone face! I'm dyin' up here!

> *THE RAM laughs, again.*

Hey, you wanna hear a joke?

ABRAHAM No.

THE RAM Sure, you do.

ABRAHAM I don't think you're funny.

THE RAM Forget your troubles with a joke!

ABRAHAM I said no.

THE RAM Have you got a better choice?

> *Pause. ABRAHAM looks at ISAAC.*

ABRAHAM Go ahead. Make me laugh.

THE RAM Great! Okay, so it's, like, ancient times and there's this guy who wants to get rich. So, he decides what he needs to do is go to Jerusalem, to the Temple they got there, and offer a sacrifice. Then ask God for the riches. Good idea, right? Great, but he doesn't know what to sacrifice. So he looks around his place. He's a poor guy. He's got a couple goats, maybe a chicken or something, but he doesn't want to part with any of that. Suddenly, he realizes in the fridge, he's got a big package of bologna. So he takes a slice of bologna, saddles his ass and travels three days to the Temple. At the altar, he burns the sacred bologna as an offering. When the bologna's all burnt he gets on his knees and says:

"My Lord, dear God, behold my offering! Now, call down to me! Bless me with the wealth of the earth, ten-fold!"

No luck. God in heaven is silent.

The guy goes home. A month passes and he's still as poor and miserable as all hell. So he decides to make another sacrifice. Saddles up his ass, and again, makes the long trip to Jerusalem. At the altar, with another slice of bologna, he makes another sacrifice. He gets on his knees and says:

"My Lord, dear God, behold my offering! Now, call down to me! Bless me with the wealth of the earth, ten-fold!"

Still no luck. The heavens are silent.

He goes home. Another month passes. Same thing. Except this time, he's kind of upset. He takes ten slices of bologna, his saddle, his ass, gets to the Temple and builds a huge bologna bonfire for the Lord, like you've never seen! Again, he says:

"My Lord, dear God, behold my offering! Now call down to me! Bless me with the wealth of the earth, tenfold!"

As usual, God is silent.

Now, this guy is enraged. Three trips he's made, three perfectly good offerings and for what? Diddly-squat. He's red in the face. The guy points his finger to the heavens and cries:

"Oh Lord, God, you have forsaken me! I have burnt you stupendous offerings, everything of value to me, and still you spurn me with silence and ignore my pleas! I spit on your altar!"

THE RAM spits.

Suddenly, the heavens part and God says:

In a very off-hand voice:

"Aaaayyyhhh, what a bunch-a bologna!

Slight pause. THE RAM laughs, guffawing and snorting. ABRAHAM steps back.

Bologna! Get it?

More laughter.

You gotta admit! I made you laugh!

*THE RAM continues to laugh, ignoring
ABRAHAM. ABRAHAM points at the sun.*

ABRAHAM   Look, Isaac. The sunset.

*ISAAC and THE RAM look at the sun. It sinks
below the horizon and disappears. As they watch,
ABRAHAM clutches his knife.*

THE RAM   Man! Those colors! It's like seeing a pink monkey!
No! A pink monkey with a purple erection! Who
could possibly believe!

*ABRAHAM reaches his knife around ISAAC and
holds it to his throat.*

ISAAC   Dad...

*ABRAHAM presses the knife against ISAAC.
ISAAC freezes. THE RAM sees them.*

THE RAM   Whoa!

THE RAM freezes.

What the hell's going on, here?

ABRAHAM   Be quiet, please.

*ABRAHAM slowly forces ISAAC down, onto his
knees.*

Look at me.

ISAAC tilts his head and looks up at his father.

I'm gonna cut your throat. I'm gonna dash your
blood on the stones and then burn your carcass.

ISAAC shakes.

Please open your life. This moment. For me.

*ISAAC looks at his father. Again, ABRAHAM
presses the knife into ISAAC's throat. ISAAC
grows calm and closes his eyes. He inhales,
exhales, and then calmly waits.*

Good, Isaac. Relax. No empty conversation. No
jokes, no distractions. Only this burden. Are you
ready? Here I am!

ABRAHAM is about to kill ISAAC.

THE RAM   Stop it!

ABRAHAM stops. Slowly, he looks at THE RAM.

Are you fucking crazy? Are you insane? What the
hell is wrong with you?

THE RAM walks over to ABRAHAM, slowly.

My God, it's like a kindergarten, over here!

*THE RAM holds out his hand, but ABRAHAM
and ISAAC stay in position.*

C'mon, champ! Gimme the knife. You need a time-
out.

They do not move.

Look. Whatever's going on, I think you're takin' it
a bit too seriously, don't you think? C'mon! Calm
down a bit, tell some jokes with the boy, have a
few laughs. Try to not look so biblical. I mean, this
is a nice camping trip. Father-son thing. The fire
and everything. Just make nice. And give me the
knife. *(pause)* C'mon, pops, hand it over.

*ABRAHAM lowers the knife. ISAAC slumps.
ABRAHAM stares at THE RAM.*

Great. Now hand it here.

ABRAHAM   Who are you?

THE RAM   What?

ABRAHAM   I asked who you are.

THE RAM   Who am I? I'm Ram! C'mon!

ABRAHAM   Why are you here?

THE RAM   What, you mean, here?

ABRAHAM   Yes.

THE RAM   Why?

> *THE RAM is befuddled.*

What, you want me to stay at home every night, picking my toes? I mean, duh! I'm here to see some things, flowers, colors, the view! Put a few jokes in and lighten up your world! You know!

> *ABRAHAM suddenly laughs. Both ISAAC and THE RAM stare at him, confused.*

Hello? Sir Psycho? What's so funny?

> *ABRAHAM steps forward with his knife. THE RAM starts to back up.*

Hey, uh, wait. What... what are you doing, there?

> *ABRAHAM thrusts his knife into THE RAM's belly and lifts it upwards, sharply. THE RAM gasps for breath and then falls to the ground. THE RAM dies. ABRAHAM's knife is covered in blood. ABRAHAM looks at ISAAC. ISAAC is shocked. ABRAHAM kneels. He then reaches down and takes some of THE RAM's blood on his hand.*

ABRAHAM   Look. Blood.

> *ABRAHAM approaches ISAAC.*

This could be you. This could be all reversed.

> *ABRAHAM smears the blood on ISAAC's face.*
> *ISAAC shakes. They look at each other.*

Oh God! Your beautiful face!

> *ABRAHAM smiles, then laughs, near tears. ISAAC*
> *tries to stand, stumbles, then sits.*

ISAAC   I... I don't feel so...

ABRAHAM   So unique!

ISAAC   You killed... you...

ABRAHAM   Look at him. He's nothing. In time, we'll forget.
(pause) But you, my son, are present. You remain.

> *ISAAC takes out a pack of cigarettes. He lights one.*
> *ISAAC smokes, shaking.*

If you want to quit smoking, I think the only way
is cold turkey.

> *ISAAC continues to shake.*

It's very bad for you to smoke.

ISAAC   Better than a knife in the gut.

ABRAHAM   That's true.

ISAAC   Better than that guy's health, that's for sure.

> *ISAAC butts out his cigarette.*

ABRAHAM   You would have let me.

ISAAC   I'd no choice...

ABRAHAM   No, you let me.

        Pause.

We need to cut him up. Then put him on the fire.

ISAAC   We do? Me?

ABRAHAM   I'll help. First, we'll build the fire.

        ISAAC looks at ABRAHAM.

It's okay. Come here.

        ISAAC gains composure, stands and goes to ABRAHAM. Together, ABRAHAM and ISAAC throw more logs on the fire.

ISAAC   Dad...

        ISAAC backs away from the fire and looks over at THE RAM's corpse. ABRAHAM turns to ISAAC.

ABRAHAM   You'll need this.

        ABRAHAM withdraws his knife and holds it out for ISAAC. ISAAC steps back.

ISAAC   I can't. Blood makes me sick.

ABRAHAM   Take it. It belongs to you. *(pause)* A gift.

        ISAAC takes the knife. He withdraws and goes to THE RAM. He kneels by the corpse and holds the knife over it. He has difficulty beginning the gruesome task.

ISAAC   Dad, I...

ABRAHAM   Amazing. Still me. Still alone.

ISAAC   How can I...

ABRAHAM   Isaac, you don't have to like me. Or feel close to me. Or forgive me. Ever. Just know I'm here. That's enough. *(pause)* I know you're here, too. *(pause)* What are you thinking?

ISAAC   I'm just listening to your voice.

    ABRAHAM smiles.

ABRAHAM   Good. *(pause)* Do you know what I'd really like, Isaac?

ISAAC   What?

ABRAHAM   Grandchildren.

ISAAC   Alright.

ABRAHAM   Now, please, cut him up.

    ISAAC looks at THE RAM. He holds the knife near the corpse, anticipating. He freezes. ABRAHAM watches the fire.

ACT TWO

> *A large family room, faintly resembling a king's royal court. Tapestries hanging, a carpet on the floor. Darkly lit. There are two entrance ways, on either side of the room. A coat rack stands in the corner, by one entrance. There are three chairs in the centre of the room, evenly spaced, facing forward. The central chair is the largest, similar to a throne. To its left sits the second chair, a smaller version of the central one. To its right sits the third chair, much plainer and smaller than the second. The chairs face a television/stereo/entertainment centre downstage, indicated. ISAAC sits in the central chair with a flowing blanket over his legs. He is an old man, wearing a pair of dark sunglasses. In front of his chair is a flimsy television table, with an ornate box and a remote control. He starts to cough. He sits still for a moment, then starts to cough, again, louder.*

ISAAC   Help! *(pause)* Help me! *(pause)* Jacob!

> *JACOB enters. He is a young man, smoking.*

Are you here?

JACOB   No.

ISAAC   You're not?

JACOB   Nope.

ISAAC   Where are you, then?

JACOB   Here.

ISAAC   Very funny. *(pause)* I need a glass of water.

JACOB   You always need something.

ISAAC   Please.

> *JACOB exits. Pause. He returns with a glass of water and hands it to ISAAC. ISAAC drinks.*

Thank you.

JACOB	It's not like I had a choice, Dad.
ISAAC	No.

JACOB starts to leave.

Will you sit with me for a moment?

JACOB	Why?
ISAAC	I'm your father and I asked you.

JACOB sits in the larger, second chair. He picks up the remote control and turns on the television.

You're smoking. *(pause)* I can smell it.

JACOB	It's not smoke. It's daisies. They really smell up a room.
ISAAC	When a man loses his sight, his other senses become more acute.
JACOB	So you say.
ISAAC	It's a fact.
JACOB	I can't prove it.
ISAAC	Your smoking, it bothers me.
JACOB	It doesn't bother me.
ISAAC	What are you doing?
JACOB	I'm watching TV.
ISAAC	That's not your chair. That's your brother's.

JACOB moves to his chair, the third. Pause.

Well?

JACOB   I'm watching TV, Dad.

ISAAC   What are you watching?

JACOB   Crap.

ISAAC   Why are you watching that?

JACOB   'Cause that's what I like to watch.

ISAAC   There are other things to do.

JACOB   Like what?

ISAAC   We could talk to each other.

JACOB   About what?

ISAAC   There are as many things to say as there are ideas in your mind.

JACOB   That sounds like the wisdom of a blind man.

ISAAC   It is the wisdom of a blind man. *(pause)* You could talk to me. We're the same flesh and blood.

JACOB   No, we're not.

ISAAC   We have the same root. *(pause)* Maybe we... I mean, we could...

JACOB   I've got nothing to say, Dad.

               ISAAC coughs again. JACOB watches.

ISAAC   Help!

JACOB   *(muttering)* Fuck. Hang on.

               JACOB grabs the glass and exits. ISAAC continues to cough. Pause. JACOB returns with more water. He hands the glass to ISAAC. ISAAC drinks.

ISAAC   Thank you.

JACOB	Right.

JACOB returns to his place.

ISAAC	Oh, Jacob. I'm not well.
JACOB	No.
ISAAC	My voice, it sounds–
JACOB	Like a car accident.
ISAAC	I'm losing my strength.
JACOB	It happens.
ISAAC	It's not coming back.
JACOB	Oh God, Dad.... *(pause)* Everyone's gotta die. Don't make it into a soap opera.

JACOB rubs out his cigarette. ISAAC sighs.

ISAAC	What time is it?
JACOB	I don't know. Evening, sometime.
ISAAC	Late afternoon.
JACOB	Whatever you want to call it.
ISAAC	Has your brother returned?
JACOB	No.
ISAAC	He's late.
JACOB	How do you know he's late, if you don't know what time it is?
ISAAC	That was a question.
JACOB	It didn't sound like a question.

ISAAC   He's definitely late.

JACOB   I'm sure he's very busy.

ISAAC   Where is he? I have to speak with him.

JACOB   About what?

ISAAC   I'm lonely, Jacob. It doesn't matter what I say. It
               only matters that I'm heard. *(pause)* I wonder what
               he's doing so late?

JACOB   He's probably on his hands and knees, vigorously
               kissing his boss's ass.

               ISAAC starts to cough.

               There's water on your table, Dad.

               ISAAC is coughing. He struggles to find the glass.

ISAAC   Help! I can't... I...

               JACOB gets up and hands ISAAC the glass.

JACOB   Here.

               *ISAAC drinks. JACOB sits. ISAAC puts the glass
               down.*

ISAAC   Ah...

               ISAAC catches his breath.

               Be nicer to your brother. He's my son. And your
               kin.

JACOB   I'm plenty nice to him.

ISAAC   No...

JACOB   I could be a hell of a lot meaner.

               Pause.

ISAAC   Could you turn off the television and play me
          some music?

          JACOB grabs the remote control and presses a
          couple of buttons. Music plays. JACOB starts
          to exit.

          Don't leave. Please. Sit and listen with me.

          JACOB sits in his chair. They listen to music.

          Ah! Where would we be without music? Blind to
          the world! In music, still, we climb and descend.
          Every moment, a note, a life, a pause. *(pause)*
          When I was your age, I was a musician.

JACOB   I know.

ISAAC   I was a professional.

JACOB   I know. And people played your compositions. But
          now you love music because you can be a blind
          invalid, and still experience the whole wide world
          just by listening, I know.

          Pause. Music.

ISAAC   So you know all my thoughts, sitting over there?

JACOB   I spend a lot of time with you.

ISAAC   That's not what I was going to say. *(pause)* I love
          music because it's never failed me. The vibration
          of a note is the experience, itself. Music doesn't
          refer to something outside of itself, a meaning out
          in the world. No. And it's because music commu-
          nicates nothing, that it can never fail in its delivery.
          It simply opens us up, right now. It makes us
          vulnerable, vigilant and awake. We're alive when
          we vibrate with it. Listen, you can hear.... *(pause)*
          You know, when I was your age, I went on a
          camping trip with my father–

JACOB   *(muttering)* Oh God...

ISAAC   We climbed a mountain together. Camped out on
               the peak. I hardly spoke to him. My father was in a
               very strange mood that evening. He was upset.
               Crazy, even. He seemed so desperate and over-
               wrought. He put a sharp knife to my throat, said
               he was going to kill me. The shock of that. You
               can't imagine. My father looked me in the eye. He
               was so present, so complete. He gave me his
               whole life with that look. Then, when my father
               spoke to me, I heard only the musicality of his
               words. I listened and we were both so open. So
               vulnerable and desperate in our skins. I wish you
               could have been there, Jacob. I don't think I've
               ever felt more alive my whole life than in that
               moment. My father was going to kill me, but I
               didn't resist.

JACOB   I know, Dad.

               Pause.

ISAAC   You know?

JACOB   You've told me that story before.

ISAAC   You know!?

JACOB   Yeah–

ISAAC   This is not something–

JACOB   Dad–

ISAAC   –not a thing that one knows!

JACOB   Okay–

ISAAC   It's not a fact or a piece of knowledge or even a
               story!

JACOB   Okay!

ISAAC   It's what I'm saying now, and what you're
               listening to!

JACOB   Fine.

ISAAC   Don't!

JACOB   You have to relax. *(pause)* I heard that story before. I could lie and tell you I haven't, but I have. More than once.

ISAAC   Jacob...

JACOB   What?

> *Long pause. Music. JACOB turns off the music and turns on the television.*

ISAAC   I'm hungry.

JACOB   I'll get you some bread.

ISAAC   Could you make me a sandwich?

JACOB   Dad... no.

ISAAC   Bread, then.

> *JACOB stands and exits. ISAAC listens to music. JACOB re-enters with a piece of bread.*

JACOB   Here.

> *JACOB hands him the bread and sits in his chair.*

ISAAC   Thank you.

> *Just as he's about to take a bite, ISAAC stops.*

Do you want this?

JACOB   No.

ISAAC   I don't mind. If you want it.

JACOB   I'm not hungry.

> *ISAAC takes a bite.*

ISAAC   It's stale.

JACOB   Yeah.

ISAAC   Still, satiating.

JACOB   There's something.

> *JACOB lights a cigarette. ISAAC eats.*

ISAAC   You're smoking.

JACOB   I know.

ISAAC   You know it hurts my breathing.

JACOB   It's a habit, Dad. I'm an addict.

ISAAC   Put it out.

JACOB   Gotta get me on one of those twelve-step programs.

ISAAC   I said–

JACOB   Okay! I heard you!

> *JACOB rubs his cigarette out.*

For fuck's sake.

ISAAC   You don't need to get–

JACOB   It's out!

> *Pause.*

ISAAC   Thank you for the bread.

JACOB   A great pleasure.

ISAAC   For all I know, this could be my final meal. *(pause)*
              There comes a time. In every life. The body's
              broken. The air's thick gravy. All light has been
              banished. This room, to me, is neither greater nor
              lesser than the peak of a tall mountain.

JACOB   Mm-hm.

ISAAC   You never know, Jacob. I might die tonight.

JACOB   I'll bet you twenty bucks you don't.

ISAAC   I don't want to die alone.

JACOB   You're not alone.

ISAAC   I might as well be. You and me, we could sit in
              the same room for eternity and still be alone. Two
              isolated islands, with no bridge between. In your
              voice, nothing but–

JACOB   Dad!

              Pause.

ISAAC   Well, a least, I have one son who reaches out. Who
              tries to meet me, face-to-face, with every word he
              speaks. I have no need to worry.

              *ISAAC puts his hand on the box in front of him.
              JACOB watches him, curiously.*

JACOB   What's in the box, Dad?

ISAAC   It doesn't concern you.

JACOB   Tell me what's in the god damn box.

ISAAC   I haven't told you yet. What makes you think I'll
              tell you now?

              *JACOB grabs the box from off the table and shakes
              it. He tries to pull on the lock.*

Why don't you throw it onto the floor and kick it a few times?

JACOB puts the box back on the table.

JACOB	Where's the key?
ISAAC	Down my pants.
JACOB	Give it to me.
ISAAC	Don't you have any respect?
JACOB	I'll break the fucking thing open if I have to.
ISAAC	My pants or the box?
JACOB	You want to test me?
ISAAC	Do it and we're forever severed. I'll curse you in my grave.
JACOB	All you're gonna do in your grave is rot.
ISAAC	Jacob! (*pause*) Well?
JACOB	Forget it.

JACOB sits and watches television.

You don't need me. Esau can kiss your ass 'til he's blue in the face. I'm not interested. Keep your damn box.

ISAAC	I don't want my ass kissed.
JACOB	I don't care.
ISAAC	All I want, Jacob... is to meet, face-to–
JACOB	Shut up!
ISAAC	Don't tell me to shut up!

JACOB   Don't fucking yell at me!

ISAAC   I'm your father!

JACOB   I'm your son! So what!

ISAAC   I'm worried about you.

JACOB   *(muttering)* Oh God...

ISAAC   The things you say...

JACOB   Then stop listening to me.

ISAAC   Why don't you work?

JACOB   I don't wanna work.

ISAAC   To break your shell. Anything. A job.

JACOB   Doing what? Filing a bunch of papers for some asshole bureaucrat? Or maybe marketing gizmos for some blood-sucking business?

ISAAC   You're so intelligent. There's school–

JACOB   Never.

ISAAC   A life of study and contemplation.

JACOB   In a world of pseudo-civilized egomaniacs who'd like nothing better than to cut each others' throats.

ISAAC   Even for yourself. Just to read.

JACOB   I like my life.

ISAAC   But all you do–

JACOB   I said I like my life!

ISAAC   All you do is sleep!

JACOB   That's all I want to do!

ISAAC	Jacob...
JACOB	I'm serious. I like to sleep. Good twelve to fourteen hour stretches. Waking up groggy with no energy to rise. So atrophied all I can do is fall back asleep.
ISAAC	That breaks my heart, Jacob.
JACOB	All the desperate people. Taking themselves so seriously. The images of discipline, hustling to and from places, picking up things, dropping off things. I prefer lying in bed. I can be myself. *(pause)* Besides, it's not all I do. I watch a lot of TV.
ISAAC	So much solipsism.
JACOB	I don't have a dictionary, Dad.
ISAAC	You're consumed by yourself. You're a circle, beginning and ending with your own self, and you learn nothing on the journey around the curves. You don't reach out. You demand nothing. You give nothing. You just sit and stew in your own meanness.
JACOB	Right.
ISAAC	You need to try. Like your brother.

JACOB grabs the clicker and turns off the television.

JACOB	Do you want some more water?
ISAAC	He speaks so beautifully! One feels lucky to hear his voice!
JACOB	I'm gonna get you another glass of water.

JACOB grabs ISAAC's glass and starts to exit.

Always great to talk to you, Dad.

JACOB exits. Pause. ISAAC sighs. He feels for the box, picks it up and puts it in his lap. JACOB enters.

I got your water. Here.

JACOB puts the water on ISAAC's table.

ISAAC	Jacob... I'm trying. I'm your father. I want only what's best for you.
JACOB	Which is what? For me to speak falsely and wear fancy suits? To always pretend, like Esau? He's all image, Dad. He's nothing but–
ISAAC	Stop it! *(pause)* Esau's very happy with his life.
JACOB	I know.
ISAAC	He has confidence. Self-respect.
JACOB	Unlike me.
ISAAC	He's the epitome of respect!
JACOB	Only assholes talk like that.
ISAAC	Pretty eloquent for an asshole.
JACOB	It's not real! Things don't fucking rhyme!
ISAAC	Your brother doesn't rhyme.
JACOB	He might as well.
ISAAC	It's a certain kind of elegant speech pattern.
JACOB	It's pretentious, dishonest, and delusional.
ISAAC	The beauty of his voice... the way that he speaks...
JACOB	I don't believe him, Dad. He's not English.
ISAAC	It's a joy to get lost in his words!

JACOB lights a cigarette.

JACOB   I don't believe you, either.

ISAAC   Please–

JACOB   I don't think you really like him.

ISAAC   –the smoke.

JACOB   And I think it's depressing, your fake fawning.

ISAAC gags.

ISAAC   I... can't...

JACOB   I need to smoke! I'm going stir crazy!

ISAAC   After I'm dead, you can smoke to your heart's content!

JACOB   The whole point is I need the nicotine right now, Dad, this second!

ISAAC coughs.

I'll get you more water.

ISAAC   *(coughing)* I don't... want...

JACOB   Fine!

JACOB drops his cigarette and vigorously rubs it out.

I can't even fucking smoke! All day I get you every fucking thing and all I want is a bit of rotten air in my lungs!

ISAAC   I'll be out of your hair soon enough!

JACOB   No, you won't.

Outside, there is the sound of a door opening and closing.

ISAAC	Your brother's home.
JACOB	You're gonna live another twenty years.
ISAAC	Not true. I'm dying, Jacob. *(pause)* All I want is to speak to you. To listen to you. For us to crack each other open and–
ESAU	*(off)* Greetings!
ISAAC	–know the other's there to hear!
JACOB	I have nothing to say! Nothing to hear, nothing to say, nothing!
ISAAC	No...
JACOB	I'm not you, Dad!

> *ESAU enters. He is dressed in serious, Elizabethan stage garb, with hints of a business suit. A cape, hat, knickers, tights He takes himself seriously, a good actor. He speaks naturally. He stands by the entrance, listening. He takes off his cape and hat and hangs them on the coat rack.*

ISAAC	You don't have to be so despairing. We could meet and–
JACOB	I hate my fucking life. My pathetic nothing life. It's a prison cell.
ISAAC	But all of us, every last one–
ESAU	Uh, father–
ISAAC	*(muttering)* Shit.
ESAU	–Sire–
ISAAC	Yes?
ESAU	–I'm home, but, what is this?

ISAAC   Nothing. Just a conversation.

                JACOB sighs.

JACOB   How's it hangin', Hamlet?

                ESAU glares at JACOB, icily.

                (in a bad British accent) Oh deeah! Did Richard
                Burbage have a bad day at the Globe?

ESAU   Dear brother, thou hast not forgot my name.
                'Tis a label I love, not some rude joke,
                Some mocking tongue toy that thou canst share
                With heroic Hamlet, Greatest of Danes,
                Or Richard Burbage, the theatre's first man
                'Pon Shakespeare's Globe stage. With these infant
                     games
                Thou mockest meaning and its sacred cloth.
                For language is but dear God's holy dress.
                And as language to God, so my name t'me;
                'Tis the sole chariot of mine own soul,
                An anchored barb for this transient flesh.
                Dear brother–

JACOB   Who the hell do you think you are?

ESAU   –thou knowest my name–

JACOB   You're not John Gielgud.

ESAU   –use it!

JACOB   This isn't London.

ESAU   And even if thy brother's sweet implore
                Dost fail to penetrate that brick-wall brain
                Thou hast erected with such thoughtless pride,
                Methinks thy father–

JACOB   You're a laughable joke!

ESAU   –so blind and chair-bound,
                Should not be witness to some mongrel bitch
                Of a cur! 'Twill not be! I give my oath!

JACOB   Don't lecture me.

ESAU   I'll speak as I see fit 'til I'm complete.
               Thy father's nothing less than thine own God,
               Thy private king and sacred fountainhead;
               A point of light in the night's cloudless sky,
               Most blesséd by the order of the stars.
               For certain thou needs be a sailor wise
               Upon life's turbulent, tortuous sea
               And know enough to turn thine eyes and chin
               Up towards this one North Star, true fixéd point,
               This father! Heed this great and steadfast man!
               His guidance in our rough-and-tumble waves
               Will surely shield us from sea storms so cruel,
               Or dashings mad upon Fate's angry rocks.

JACOB   Don't condescend to me, you prick.

ESAU   'Tis not what thou calls condescension, this.
               For when a human speaks with brutish beast—

ISAAC   Esau!

               JACOB sits in ESAU's chair.

ESAU   O dog! The chair's not thine! Hop off, I say
               And hence unto thine infant kennel bed!

ISAAC   That's enough from both of you!

               JACOB stands.

JACOB   I think you got your tights on a little tight, there,
               cowboy.

ISAAC   Quiet!

               JACOB sits in his own chair. ESAU sits in his.

ESAU   But soft, I lose myself in ruddy rage.
               How fares thee, father, on this winter's day?

ISAAC   Not well, Esau. Please, come here.

> *ESAU kneels. ISAAC touches his face and then pulls him close into an embrace.*

My son!

ESAU   Now, father, please! While 'tis the greatest gift
To be embraced by such a loving sire
I'm still a man who doth have need of air!

ISAAC   Yes. Alright.

> *ISAAC releases ESAU.*

ESAU   I thank thee, sire, for such warm welcoming!
It's just methinks thy clasping, vice-grip joy
More fits the breathless and teary-eyed thanks
Of a prisoner, pardoned near to death;
Or fits that ancient greeting 'tween two Greeks
Odysseus, our hero lost at sea
And Telemachos, precious son ne'er seen,
Than fits this most banal return tonight:
Thy son's release from his stock market toil.

ISAAC   Of course.

ESAU   Thou hast my great respect. 'Tis solid, that,
Not washed away in slob'ring waves of hugs,
Like woman's love, or panting tongues of dogs.

ISAAC   I apologize.

ESAU   Pray tell: Hast thou much hunger? Thou hast et?

ISAAC   I had a slice of bread.

ESAU   But surely, no! Just bread and bread, alone?!

JACOB   That's all he wanted.

ESAU   Thou liest, lazy and second-born son!
Hadst thou the will to work of decent men
Thy father would feed on a feast of meat
And not the empty shells of sandwich bread.

ISAAC   It's alright.

JACOB   Make him a sandwich, yourself.

ISAAC   It doesn't matter.

ESAU   It matters much! I will not let it slide!
         'Tis a grim human fact: thou needst to eat.
         Ay, father. Man is not pure soul alone,
         For there's the omnipresent body-flesh,
         An engine always idle, burning fuel,
         With hunger pangs the empty symbol light.
         And if thou dost not fill thy fleshly tank,
         Thou shalt indeed breakdown upon life's road.

JACOB   Then perhaps Sir Laurence Olivier should getteth
         off his ass and maketh Dad an omelet.

ESAU   Have I Sir Laurence Olivier's face?
         Nay, kin. That actor's face hath decomposed
         Since he is dead, and I am not his twin.

JACOB   Then why are you talking like him?

ESAU   But wouldst thou likest a fresh omelet, sire?

ISAAC   Thank you, no. I won't be needing it.

ESAU   Methinks thou needeth this omelet, indeed.
         Two eggs, well-scrambled and mixéd with meat,
         With mushrooms and onions, and fresh goat
             cheese.
         Why, a symbol of life is th'hard-shelled egg!
         'Tis life not lived, but fed, so thou mayst live.
         But such feedings doth more than fill thy tank,
         They say: I love thy life. I'll do it, thus.

         ESAU takes ISAAC's hand, with a royal gesture,
         looking at JACOB.

         And you, take heed of this genuine act!
         I labour now for father's supper dish
         And thus do weave a sacred cord betwixt
         This father and his fav'rite rightful son,

A cord that thou, most vile, would brazen cut.
Sweet tendon 'tween two generations' flesh,
A fatal cut, so like Achilles' heel.

JACOB   I'll be sure to take heed, then. Thanks.

ESAU   He jokes! Fie, you pig!–

JACOB   It's an important lesson.

ESAU   –A pox on you!

JACOB   Maybe I can still be redeemed.

ESAU   A pox, I say! No need to humour fools.
            To kitchen, thus. I'll cooketh now thy meal.

            ESAU exits.

JACOB   What an asshole.

ISAAC   Jacob! Don't!

JACOB   He just put a fucking pox on me.

ISAAC   You've angered him!

JACOB   God damn pox wiped out half the world.

ISAAC   You're angering me! He's my son!

JACOB   Oh, stop it, Dad!

ISAAC   I will not!

JACOB   I don't believe you're angry for a second, so just
            stop!

            Pause.

ISAAC   Amazing that you're from the same womb as your
            brother. His twin. My child. *(pause)* Why do I
            waste my time? I should just face the facts. Esau's
            better than you. More intelligent, more articulate.

His poetic words are nothing more than the pale reflection of his love for me. One can hear it in his voice. *(pause)* You, Jacob, are a sour, silent, misanthropic man. You think of me as a prison sentence, not a father to love. And I'd just as soon give you your pardon. *(pause)* Well? What do you have to say for yourself?

JACOB   Nothing.

ISAAC   Nothing?

JACOB   Nothing.

ISAAC   Then I don't think I have anything else to say to you.

> *Pause. ISAAC puts the box on his lap.*

Where's your brother?

JACOB   Making you an omelet.

ISAAC   Get him.

JACOB   Why?

ISAAC   It's none of your business. *(pause)* I said get him!

> *JACOB crosses to exit. He stops. Pause. He quietly takes ESAU's discarded cape and hat from off the coat rack. Pause. JACOB puts on the hat, and then the cape. As he is doing this, ISAAC listens intently.*

Esau?

> *JACOB steps forward.*

JACOB   Here I am.

ISAAC   Esau, is that you?

JACOB   I am indeed thy dearest son, most loved,
The child that's favoured by tradition's choice
And by thy grace and will, O noble sire,
Since thou doth see such good in lineage.

ISAAC   Come here.

JACOB   Dear father, thou hast called upon thy son
With voice as sweet to me as Siren song.

ISAAC   Are we alone? Your brother, he's in the kitchen,
I assume?

JACOB   Ay, sir.

ISAAC   Good. I... I'm not well. I'm so alone. Come... let
me...

                JACOB steps closer. ISAAC reaches out and feels
                JACOB's cape and hat. ISAAC smiles.

        My well-suited son. *(pause)* Isn't it?

JACOB   Well-suited, yes! Methinks that age hath stole
Thy sight alone (and the spring from thy step)
But time hath left thy mind's command
Like a tyrant on watch against attack.
Thou hast upheld thy signature of strength:
True wit! This wond'rous reign of "well-suited"
        puns!

ISAAC   Your voice. Is something wrong?

JACOB   No, sire.

ISAAC   But your voice–

JACOB   Trust not this voice. 'Tis a watery sound
In constant flux; one ne'er can touch such things.
Know I'm thy son.

ISAAC   I understand. Kneel before me.

> *JACOB kneels before ISAAC. ISAAC touches his arm and sighs.*

How I wish we could take off our masks.

> *ISAAC removes his glasses.*

So old. Here I am.

> *ISAAC stares at JACOB. JACOB is startled. ISAAC puts his glasses on, again.*

I would give you my life, you know. I would offer it up. For you.

JACOB   But sire, for sure thy life's thy very own.

ISAAC   No. It's yours. It always has been. It's a condition of birth. We are for each other, in perpetual debt. *(pause)* I have a key. To open this box...

> *ISAAC removes the key. He picks up the box and unlocks it.*

I'm dying. Soon. No matter what I do, I'll die alone. I want to pass you this, my beautiful debt. *(pause)* All these years... with you, with your brother, I've always felt alone. Jacob... he's cruel and closed. Esau... although the speech is beautiful, so beautiful, it never lets the guard down. You hide, my son, behind Elizabethan flourishes. A cloaking style that's never honest, never true to this moment, right here, right now, between us. I have never been met, face-to-face, by my sons. The way my father once met me. *(pause)* I wonder... could we break each other's shell? Could we take off our masks? Could you give me your most prized possession, as a bridge, so that I could pass you this, and finally die free of debt? I did the same for my father.

JACOB   Whatever's thy request I'll surely do.

> *ISAAC opens the box and pulls out the knife.*

ISAAC   Only this.

> *ISAAC holds up the knife.*

Let me cut your tongue.

JACOB   What?

ISAAC   Your fancy speech, severed, forever. *(pause)* Well?

> *Pause. JACOB kneels in front of ISAAC. He moves closer and takes ISAAC's hand. ISAAC puts his arm around JACOB's head. JACOB trembles, but doesn't resist. With the knife, ISAAC cuts off the tip of JACOB's tongue.*

JACOB   Ah!

> *JACOB falls back. His mouth is bloody.*

ISAAC   My son!

JACOB   *(muffled)* Oh God! My tongue!

ISAAC   Only the skin off the tip.

> *JACOB coughs blood. Pause.*

Are you alright?

JACOB   *(muffled)* Yes.

ISAAC   You let me.

> *Pause. ISAAC holds out the knife.*

Here. Take this. Your gift.

> *JACOB takes the knife.*

Speak to me! With your real voice!

> *Pause.*

JACOB	I don't have anything to say.
ISAAC	Listen to your voice! My son, so unique!

ESAU enters, holding a omelet. He stops.

ESAU	Good sir! All's well? My kin doth bleed from lips!
	Why doth he wear my jacket and my hat?
	But pray, what scuff hath just ensued this eve?
	Do tell! I'll sure crusade thy holy cause!
ISAAC	Esau?

ESAU steps forward.

ESAU	What ails thee, sire? 'Tis an ashen gray hue
	That spreads like wanton rash upon thy face.
ISAAC	Sit down.

ESAU sits. He puts the omelet on ISAAC's television table.

The way you speak. It's very beautiful, Esau. I've always loved it.

ESAU	Ay, sir, I know. 'Tis for thy pleasure done.
	'Tis for the look of satisfaction, sire,
	Which says thou knowest you've a noble son.
	Thy Jacob's speech is just a whimsy garb,
	He wears it with such vanity and pride,
	Like fawning frills of taffeta and lace
	Upon some girlish harlot's haughty dress!
	Not me! From my throat flows the rhythmic bard,
	Our poet Shakespeare's manly voice, most deep,
	Which echoes far and wide from mouths of kings,
	And from the throne's defenders 'pon wild shores!
	A testament to you, my precious sire!
	A banner, proudly waving father's line.
ISAAC	Come here, Esau. Kneel.

ESAU kneels before ISAAC.

Today, I've given your brother a gift. But I have
nothing for you. To you, I can offer only advice.
Respect your brother's gift. He is strong because of
it. Don't be angry at him. Rather, bless him for his
strength, and you will find your own. *(pause)*
There. That's all.

ESAU is stunned.

Your brother was here before you. I gave him the
box on my table. Your box. I have treated him as
I would've you. *(pause)* I'm sorry.

ESAU   Suh... suh...

ISAAC   What's done is done.

ESAU   Selfish! Godless!

ISAAC   Now, wait–

ESAU   Bastard! Cur!

ISAAC   Just a moment, Esau!

ESAU   O brother...

ESAU faces JACOB.

ISAAC   Even your Shakespeare willed his wife, Hathaway,
the second best bed.

ESAU   Thou hast unchained the beast inside the cage!

ISAAC   Perhaps second best is not always what it seems.

ESAU   O, like a wolf I'll hunt thee by the moon,
'Til when I catch thee, kin, with canine claws–

ISAAC   Not everyone's fit for the first best bed!

ESAU   I'll cut and rip thine entrails into shreds
And scatter them upon the forest floor.

ISAAC	Esau!
ESAU	Thou shalt not live!
ISAAC	Listen to me!

JACOB steps forward. He speaks with a slight lisp.

JACOB	He can't hear you, Dad.
ESAU	O dev'lish child, thou didst a grievous wrong! 'Tis 'gainst the stream of nature's righteous flow! A futile swim, for I'm the 'pointed son.

JACOB lights a cigarette.

JACOB	My tongue was cut, not yours.
ESAU	Smoke thy fag. 'Tis thy final act in life.

ESAU approaches JACOB. JACOB pulls out the knife, stopping him.

JACOB	Back off. Keep away from me.
ESAU	Thy threats are thin. They'll crack and break in time.
JACOB	I'm serious.
ESAU	No. Now thy life's an ever-wakeful watch For if thou drifts into the land of dreams I'll steal thy knife and bleed thee from thy neck. Ne'er shall thou waketh from eternal sleep.
JACOB	Dad, are you gonna stand for this?
ISAAC	No, I won't. It's time for you to leave.
JACOB	What?
ISAAC	Go, Jacob.
JACOB	What are you talking about?

ISAAC   Take your knife. Leave us alone.

JACOB   I... I don't want to.

ISAAC   You should be on your own. Esau will stay. He'll have my money. And my home.

JACOB   Dad...

ISAAC   You'll do fine. I know it.

> *Long pause. JACOB lowers the knife and looks at ESAU.*

JACOB   Listen to you. Fancy words. Beautiful lies. All your eloquent bullshit. A shell, never dented, never showing a crack. Down to each and every syllable.

ESAU   O yes. Take pride in thy vulgarity.
For when thou diest 'pon a flea-bit bed
Vulgarity will 'company thy death.

JACOB   Probably.

ESAU   Get out!

JACOB   Fine.

> *JACOB goes to the entrance.*

Guess I won't be needing this anymore.

> *JACOB takes off his hat and cape leaves them on the coat rack. He hovers by the exit.*

JACOB   So. Guess that's it, then, huh?

ESAU   I curse thee, pig, and curse thee once again.
To hell with thee, where mayst thou burn in flames.

JACOB   Dad–

ISAAC   Good-bye, Jacob.

JACOB exits.

ESAU　　Father! My knife!

ISAAC　　My dear little boy. Come here.

ESAU kneels by ISAAC's chair, head down. ISAAC picks up the omelet.

ESAU　　Ne'er shall I leave thee, sire. I'm here, alone.
Alone I'll stay with thee for all of time.

ISAAC　　Yes, Esau. I know.

ISAAC eats.

ACT THREE

> *A drab, bureaucratic office. A table and two chairs, gray, colorless light. A small window. Any decoration is minimal, and uninteresting. There are two doors, on either side of the room. On one, a sign reads: "No entry. Official use only." JOSEPH, a young man, stands reading information from a clipboard. He looks up from the clipboard, disturbed.*

JOSEPH   Oh God.

> *JOSEPH is completely struck. Pause. There is a knocking on the door. JOSEPH composes himself, returns to his notes and looks up. JACOB, now an elderly man, peeks into the room. He is shabby, and speaks with a very slight lisp; the tip of his tongue is cut. JOSEPH doesn't look at him.*

JACOB   Uh... hello?

JOSEPH   Yes?

JACOB   Is this...

JOSEPH   Yes.

JACOB   I have an appointment for–

> *JACOB looks at his watch.*

JOSEPH   I know. You're on time.

JACOB   Oh. Okay. Well, here I am.

> *JACOB enters the room. He is holding a small box, close to him. He holds up the box.*

I brought a gift. For your employer. A very special gift. *(pause)* Are you... *(pause)* Are you ready for–?

JOSEPH   I'm ready. Please sit down.

> *JACOB sits. He puts the box on the table.*

	Name.
JACOB	What?
JOSEPH	Your name.
JACOB	Jacob.
JOSEPH	Occupation.
JACOB	Uh... I... I'm a...
JOSEPH	Occupation.
JACOB	I'm not consistently–
JOSEPH	When you've worked in the past, what have you done?
JACOB	A number of things.
JOSEPH	Name something.
JACOB	I sold tires.
JOSEPH	Tires.
JACOB	Recycled tires.
JOSEPH	When.
JACOB	Uh...

Pause.

| JOSEPH | I said when. |
| JACOB | I know. |

JOSEPH turns to JACOB. They stare at each other. Long pause.

| JOSEPH | You're not cooperating. |

JACOB	No. I'm sorry, I–
JOSEPH	Jacob, is it? There's something you should understand. As much as my employer would like to help people in your situation, he has limited time. Certainly none to whittle away. That's why we have a procedure. And that's why you must respect it. We can't help applicants who won't answer our questions.
JACOB	Yes, of course, I... I understand...
JOSEPH	Again, sir, when were you employed in the above-mentioned retail of used tires?
JACOB	Thirty-six years ago.
JOSEPH	And how long were you employed in this position?
JACOB	Six days.
JOSEPH	Excuse me?
JACOB	Well, five and a half, really.
JOSEPH	Five days?
JACOB	Five full days and one terrible morning.
JOSEPH	You worked for five days selling tires some thirty-six years ago?
JACOB	Yes, that's correct.
JOSEPH	This is the profession you would like to have reported to my employer?
JACOB	I don't like stupid jobs.
JOSEPH	And that's–
JACOB	–that's all there is out there.

JOSEPH	—so you—
JACOB	I haven't worked since.
JOSEPH	—that's for thirty-six years.
JACOB	Jobs. They crush your soul. The whole God damn system.
JOSEPH	I see. But now you simply think—
JACOB	No work, no profession. I made my own way.
JOSEPH	—you think my employer is the kind of man who just—
JACOB	Yes, I do.
JOSEPH	Oh?
JACOB	Why not?
JOSEPH	My employer is not a charity.
JACOB	He isn't?
JOSEPH	He demands certain reasonable sacrifices from applicants.
JACOB	I know. I brought him a gift.
JOSEPH	If you haven't worked for so long, how have you lived?
JACOB	I stole food for a while. Then borrowed some money. Eventually, I married rich.
JOSEPH	I see.
JACOB	Pretty fucking smart, huh?
JOSEPH	Very clever.
JACOB	And now—

JOSEPH	Now you want a hand-out from my employer.
JACOB	He's the one who advertised.
JOSEPH	Yes.
JACOB	I saw his ads. All over the place. "Feeling famished? Farrow's got bread! One small fee!" Catchy. You think of that?
JOSEPH	Yes, I did.
JACOB	A multi-talented man.
JOSEPH	What happened to your rich wife?
JACOB	Mm...
JOSEPH	Dead?
JACOB	Both dead and broke.
JOSEPH	Her fortune?
JACOB	Like everybody else's.
JOSEPH	Of course.
JACOB	We were smart. We had it all invested.
JOSEPH	The collapse hit you hard.
JACOB	I didn't much care, either way.
JOSEPH	Not much foresight–
JACOB	Well, I'm no prophet.
JOSEPH	If I may be frank.
JACOB	You may, indeed, be frank.
JOSEPH	So many of you types.

JACOB	What types?
JOSEPH	The once rich. The lazy and proud. Now crawling in on your hands and knees begging for a piddly pocket of cash.
JACOB	Well, we're desperate and starving.
JOSEPH	Yes.
JACOB	We didn't have the brilliant foresight of your employer, now, did we?
JOSEPH	Apparently not.

Pause.

JACOB	May I make a request?
JOSEPH	Sure.
JACOB	I'd prefer my charity cash without a morality lesson.

Pause. JOSEPH takes notes.

Wait. I'm... I apologize. That wasn't–

JOSEPH	No.
JACOB	I'm not accustomed–
JOSEPH	Few of you are.
JACOB	I don't like bureaucracy. I shouldn't take it out on you.
JOSEPH	Say no more on the subject.
JACOB	Alright.

Pause. JOSEPH takes further notes.

Your employer. What's he like?

JOSEPH	Excuse me?
JACOB	There're so many rumours going around.
JOSEPH	So I hear.
JACOB	He must be pretty smart, huh?
JOSEPH	My employer is a very private man.
JACOB	A genius. It's like he practically knew the future. *(pause)* He's a big man? *(pause)* I heard he was big. With bright eyes. They say you can tell a genius by the eyes. Your employer's no exception.
JOSEPH	We're not here to gossip, are we?

They smile at each other, politely.

JACOB	I am curious, though. I wonder: when you work for this man, the most powerful man in the world, what's the cost? I mean, to you, personally? You are Mister Farrow's greatness, sitting there in his role. But doesn't that prevent you from meeting other people, face-to-face? How can you ever really speak to someone, really listen to him, let alone satisfy his needs? You are Mister Farrow's representative, so great. We, the applicants, are so small. We're but shadows to your stature. Tell me, how do you break that shell?
JOSEPH	Sir, I don't think this is the time–
JACOB	Right...
JOSEPH	My psychology really isn't the point.
JACOB	No. *(pause)* It's all about giving me the money.
JOSEPH	We have a procedure.
JACOB	Gimme, gimme.
JOSEPH	In due course, we might.

JACOB	I'm sorry, I was just thinking.
JOSEPH	That's allowed.
JACOB	About you.

Pause.

JOSEPH	I've worked for my employer for many years. Long before his present financial situation and world-wide fame.
JACOB	So you could, then–?
JOSEPH	What?
JACOB	You could crack–
JOSEPH	No.
JACOB	–and open.

Pause.

JOSEPH	May we please–
JACOB	Absolutely.
JOSEPH	–return to the questionnaire, please?
JACOB	Yes. Of course.

Pause.

JOSEPH	You haven't worked for thirty-six years. A kind of protest, I suppose?
JACOB	No. I'm just very lazy.
JOSEPH	That's a kind of protest, I think.
JACOB	Well, if you want to be generous, yes. *(pause)* Look. I'm not gonna make any excuses. I've lived by my own rules.

JOSEPH	Many people do.
JACOB	It might seem selfish or cruel. But I know how to give. When the time is right.
JOSEPH	Do you?
JACOB	Yes, I do.
JOSEPH	Good. Mister Farrow requires it.
JACOB	I know he does.
JOSEPH	I need to know about your family. For the questionnaire.
JACOB	I'm a widower, like I said.
JOSEPH	Siblings, parents.
JACOB	My parents are long dead. Least I think so. I haven't... well... my father. I had a break with my father. Many years ago.
JOSEPH	I see.
JACOB	It was a good thing, actually. For the both of us. I think he died a happy man.

    JACOB smiles.

JOSEPH	You have siblings?
JACOB	Yeah. I have a brother. I think he's dead, too, but I don't know for sure. Haven't seen him in years.

    JOSEPH takes notes.

He had his limitations. My brother.

    JOSEPH looks up.

JOSEPH	What limitations?

JACOB   Hard to say. He was scared, I think. Always hiding behind his language. Always respectful and firm. Always generous. But never really showing the human underneath.

JOSEPH   Right.

JACOB   Sound familiar?

JOSEPH   Should it?

JACOB   You tell me.

               Pause.

JOSEPH   Do you have any children?

JACOB   Twelve sons and one daughter.

JOSEPH   A whole gaggle.

JACOB   Assholes, unfortunately.

JOSEPH   Really?

JACOB   Probably sell your soul if they could get a couple quarters out of it.

JOSEPH   Right.

JACOB   Haven't seen any of them in years. We never speak. Don't miss them, either. *(pause)* I mean... not all of them... one of them's...

JOSEPH   No longer–?

JACOB   Yeah. When he was young.

JOSEPH   Passed away?

JACOB   I call it "dead". *(pause)* I loved him, my son. He was a good kid. Not like the others.

JOSEPH   I... I see...

JACOB	Killed in a freak accident. Long time ago. At least according to the tale his brothers told me. Some camping trip. An angry grizzly bear. They brought me his bloody clothes. No body. Just the clothes.
JOSEPH	Oh...
JACOB	I never had a chance. I mean to really talk to him. *(pause)* He died as a child. Before I could tell him... before we could connect...
JOSEPH	That's too bad.
JACOB	That's life. *(pause)* There would've been nothing to say, anyway.
JOSEPH	Really?
JACOB	What's to say? Life is a gift. To look at your child's face, that's a gift. The rest is just talk.
JOSEPH	You believe that?
JACOB	I don't know. Maybe. *(pause)* My poor Joseph. Still, the thought makes me–
JOSEPH	Yes.
JACOB	–just a bit–
JOSEPH	I'm sorry, would you–
JACOB	Hm?
JOSEPH	Would you excuse me for a second, sir?
JACOB	Uh, sure, I–
JOSEPH	I'll just be a moment.
JACOB	Alright.

JOSEPH stands and exits through the door for "official use". He leaves his clipboard. JACOB sits in the chair. He opens the box and stares at his knife. Pause. He sighs. JOSEPH re-enters the room. JACOB closes the box.

JOSEPH   Sorry about that.

JACOB   Is there a problem?

JOSEPH   No.

Pause. JOSEPH takes notes.

So your children are all grown. And, for better or worse, on their own.

JACOB   That's right.

JOSEPH   You have no dependents.

JACOB   All I need is money for one.

JOSEPH continues writing.

May I ask... is it possible to meet your employer?

JOSEPH   No. I'm afraid not.

JACOB   But I would really like it if–

JOSEPH   He never consults with clients.

JACOB   I don't believe he exists.

JOSEPH stops writing and looks up.

I think it's bullshit. Never seen a picture of the guy. Don't know anyone who's met him. It's some kind of bureaucratic hoax. Some big brother thing. That's what I think.

JOSEPH   I assure you, he exists.

JACOB   What kind of person knows the future?

JOSEPH	A lucky one.
JACOB	What kind of human understands enough to succeed where the rest of the world has failed? I'll tell you who. A fantasy person. A cover-up doll. You're hiding a massive governmental coup.
JOSEPH	That's a very colourful interpretation.
JACOB	I'll bet it's the truth.
JOSEPH	Believe what you will.

Pause. JOSEPH writes.

JACOB	So, what do you think? Do I have money coming my way?
JOSEPH	Too early to tell. We need to finish your application and process it.
JACOB	I need the money badly. I'm starving.
JOSEPH	I know.
JACOB	I have nothing. *(pause)* I'm not materialistic, really. Couldn't give two shits. Just the basics, that's all.
JOSEPH	I'll note that down.
JACOB	In fact, anything I get, I'd–
JOSEPH	*(writing)* "Not materialistic."
JACOB	*(muttering)* –give it all up–
JOSEPH	My employer appreciates modest people, like yourself.
JACOB	*(muttering)* –if my son asked.
JOSEPH	I'm sorry, did you say something?

Pause.

JACOB	No. I didn't.
JOSEPH	No job. No dependents. That's good. Now, I need to ask–
JACOB	Yes.
JOSEPH	–as part of our policy.
JACOB	Of course.
JOSEPH	What do you plan to give my employer as a token of your appreciation?
JACOB	Well, I brought him a gift.
JOSEPH	May I see it, please?
JACOB	No.
JOSEPH	Excuse me?
JACOB	It's just... it's very private. I don't want to show you.
JOSEPH	Still...
JACOB	It's an heirloom. Been in my family for generations.
JOSEPH	I need to check it over. Register it in our files. It's a matter of policy, you understand.
JACOB	I do. But I need to give it to Mister Farrow, personally. Just to make sure. It's my only prized possession.
JOSEPH	I see.
JACOB	There must be some way–
JOSEPH	It's a strict policy rule.
JACOB	But of course you can–

JOSEPH   No, I can't.

                        Pause.

JACOB   It's important, you see. You can't just put it in some warehouse with all the other trinkets and trash. Farrow has to know it's special. It's a very treasured gift.

                        JOSEPH takes notes.

                        I have a responsibility to my father.

JOSEPH   You understand, sir, unless I follow procedure I won't be able to recommend your application.

JACOB   Wait a minute!

JOSEPH   There're rules you're asking me to break.

JACOB   Right. *(pause)* Against your procedure. "Sir" at the right times. Yes, sir, had a job. Worked a certain number of days, got a brother and a dog, oh yes, love Mister Farrow, here's my favorite pair of shoes. And give my only thing. Put it in the pile with the others. All according to formal procedure. What a waste of words. What a criminal waste of your life.

JOSEPH   So what would you prefer?

                        Through the "official entry" door, FARROW shuffles into the room, slowly. He's an old man, wearing once expensive clothes that are now destroyed. A drab gray shirt and pants. His pants are held up by a rope. His skin is pale and he has longish, stringy white hair that hangs around his head from under a beat-up bowler hat. He wears a long, expensive, regal coat, that's grown old and dusty. In all, he looks profoundly tired and thoroughly defeated, echoes of a Beckett clown. JACOB and JOSEPH turn when FARROW enters. JOSEPH stands, abruptly. FARROW shuffles over to the desk and picks up JOSEPH's clipboard. He

> *looks at it. Pause. He adjusts the clipboard and squints to see better, holding it very close. Pause. He looks up at JACOB. Pause. He looks back at the board. Pause. He looks up again at JACOB, squinting and leaning forward.*

JACOB   Uh, hello.

> *FARROW looks back at the board. Pause. He puts the notes down and exits the way he entered.*

Who's the old cocker?

JOSEPH   My employer, Mister Farrow.

> *FARROW re-enters, holding a large eyeglass case. He shuffles to the desk and stops. He squints at JACOB, then opens the eyeglass case. Inside the case, there is a candy bar. FARROW is surprised. He picks up the candy bar and examines it, squinting. He sticks it in his mouth and sucks on it. FARROW removes a pair of large, coke-bottle eyeglasses, also from the case. He puts them on and looks at JACOB. Pause.*

JACOB   Hi.

> *FARROW picks up the clipboard and looks at the notes. Pause. He puts the clipboard down. He looks up at JACOB, removes the candy bar from his mouth and holds it in his hand.*

FARROW   Hm.

JOSEPH   A prospective client, sir.

FARROW   Jacob!

JACOB   That's right.

> *FARROW takes a bite of his candy bar and chews it like cud. He swallows, then puts the half-eaten candy bar back into his eyeglass case. He returns the glasses to the case as well, and then closes it. He starts to shuffle out the way he entered.*

JOSEPH   Sir, are you alright?

                FARROW stops. Pause. FARROW sighs.

                Sir?

                *FARROW turns and stares at JACOB. He leans
                forward and squints.*

JACOB   Mister Farrow, I'm very pleased to meet you. My
                name's—

FARROW   Jacob!

JACOB   Yes...

                *FARROW laughs, then stops. Pause. FARROW
                shuffles down stage and faces out. Pause.*

FARROW   Chair!

                *JOSEPH grabs his chair and puts it behind
                FARROW. FARROW sits. Pause.*

JACOB   I... I appreciate your generosity.

                *FARROW laughs, then stops. Pause. He stands
                and takes a step forward.*

FARROW   Chair!

                *JOSEPH moves the chair a step forward. FARROW
                sits, again. Pause.*

                Hat!

                JOSEPH removes FARROW's hat.

                Dim, I say. Both prospects and people. Jacob now,
                but before, another. And another, another. Each
                with the family gift. Heirlooms, prize niblets. All
                crumble and fade into Farrow. One wonders.
                Why's the... what's the point? Give 'em the bones,
                I thought for a while.

FARROW laughs, stops.

Thought!

FARROW laughs, stops.

Mistake, that. Taxes the brain for naught. Still, once thought: might they even fancy Farrow? Little lobsters, spared from pot! Ha! Cloudy brain, there. Only gave a bit of bread. Then sucked and savored their gifts! The marrow of their souls! *(pause)* Hm! *(pause)* No. Better without. Me, bathed in bubbly. Caviar and prime roast beef. Finer things. *(pause)* Nothing, really, this. Bits of brightness. Can't cure the gray. Ah! Such gray, today! *(pause)* Hat!

JOSEPH puts the hat back on FARROW's head.

JACOB   What the hell is going on here?

JOSEPH   I don't know. I... he's never done this before.

FARROW   Hat!

JOSEPH removes FARROW's hat.

Done, then. With steep waves of cash. Suck back the life support. Yes. Great joke, this. Keeping the corpse alive! Saccharine for sour lives!

FARROW laughs, stops.

A better thought: let 'em rot. *(pause)* Hat!

JOSEPH puts FARROW's hat back on his head.

JACOB   What's this, he's–?

JOSEPH   Jacob.

JACOB   –he's done? He's not giving any more money? What's wrong?

JOSEPH   Would you mind stepping outside for a moment, please?

JACOB   No. I...

> *JOSEPH hands JACOB his box from the desk.*
> *JACOB exits. JOSEPH stands beside FARROW.*

JOSEPH   Mister Farrow, sir, is everything alright? *(pause)* You had a change of mind. I understand. Frankly, sometimes I also wonder about this... charity. You give them life, of course, but what you take... they have no choice.... *(pause)* It's my opinion, sir, that we should continue to process the applications we've already taken in. And, if you'd like, we won't accept any additional ones. Slowly wind down the operation. I just don't think it's fair, otherwise. *(pause)* That man... Jacob.... *(pause)* Sir, you took me in when I had nothing. I can't thank you enough. You've been so good to me.

FARROW   Ha!

> *Pause.*

JOSEPH   He's my father. I haven't seen him since I was a boy. We were separated. I didn't even know he was alive before today.

> *FARROW turns away, slightly.*

Sir, his application is incomplete. He... he's brought no gift for you. I'm afraid I can't, officially, recommend we give him money.

FARROW   Hat!

> *JOSEPH takes the hat from FARROW's head.*

A father.

> *FARROW sighs.*

A son.

FARROW sighs.

Not alone in that. Could've, myself, with these loins. Had a rise or two in its day. Yes. Probably still could, if put to the test. Maybe. Not too late. Find a friend with proper parts. Complimentary. Together. Touching, then. Put some spunk back in the world!

FARROW laughs.

Spunk!

FARROW laughs. Pause.

Forget that. Passing on the great chain. Each person a link. Wailing, hunger-creeping decay. Great shackles, ha! No, I say. Let it break! Better to end alone. To sit and chew in silence. Spare a son from this hell. Isolation of the ages. Singularity of soul. All of it, ending now, with Farrow. Yes. Close the shades and wait. Could be, perhaps, Farrow's finest gift!

JOSEPH   You can't mean that, sir.

FARROW   What?

JOSEPH   That's terrible.

FARROW   Enough!

FARROW shakes.

None out of you!

JOSEPH   I'm sorry.

FARROW   Hat!

JOSEPH stands, holding FARROW's hat.

Hat! Hat!

> *JOSEPH slowly puts the hat on FARROW's head.*

JOSEPH   Sir, I...

> *Pause. JOSEPH pulls out the second chair, moves it next to FARROW and sits.*

I want to give him cash. A full grant. And give him a place to live. I want you to write him a cheque.

FARROW   No gift?

JOSEPH   Nothing.

FARROW   Hm.

JOSEPH   But I could offer you a gift for him. I'll give you another seven years of service. In exchange.

FARROW   Hm...

JOSEPH   Mister Farrow?

FARROW   Hat!

> *JOSEPH removes FARROW's hat.*

Service. Yes.

JOSEPH   Thank you, sir. Thank you very much.

FARROW   Service. For life.

> *Pause.*

JOSEPH   All right.

FARROW   Your children, too.

JOSEPH   I don't have children, sir.

FARROW   Someday might. Simple exchange. Father for sons. *(pause)* Yes! Paper!

> *JOSEPH slowly takes his clipboard and a pen from the table and hands them to FARROW. FARROW writes.*

Forever... mine... *(pause)* Sign!

> *JOSEPH takes the pen from FARROW and signs. FARROW looks at the signature. He puts the clipboard down.*

Chequebook!

> *JOSEPH grabs a chequebook from the table. He stands over FARROW as FARROW writes the cheque. FARROW rips it out of the book and hands it to JOSEPH.*

JOSEPH   Sir, thank you. It's extremely generous.

> *FARROW stands.*

FARROW   Chair!

> *JOSEPH grabs the chair and puts it back, next to the table.*

Give him a place. In Goshen. Ushered away. Fed, clothed, what have you. And after, board up these windows. Remove the catheter. Nothing, then. A chair, perhaps. A chair! And silence! *(pause)* Hat!

> *JOSEPH returns FARROW's hat to his head. FARROW shuffles towards the "official entry" door. On his way out, he stops near JACOB and kisses him, quickly, emotionlessly.*

Mine!

> *FARROW exits. JOSEPH goes to the other door and calls to JACOB.*

JOSEPH   Please, come in.

JACOB enters with the box and stands across from JOSEPH.

JACOB   So that's it, huh? He's done with giving. No more money.

JOSEPH   Yes, he's finished.

JACOB   Fuck.

JOSEPH   But I do have a cheque for you.

JOSEPH hands JACOB the cheque. JACOB stares at it.

Mister Farrow has also given you use of a small place in Goshen. To live. It's not the best neighbourhood, I know. But the rent is free. You can live your life there. And you can keep your heirloom. Your precious gift.

JACOB stares at JOSEPH.

I'm very happy for you.

JACOB   Thank you. *(pause)* I would give this all up, you know.

JOSEPH   You don't have to.

JACOB   I'd even die to hug my son.

JOSEPH   Yes, well. There are some things that Mister Farrow's money can't provide.

Pause. JACOB folds his cheque and puts it in his pocket.

JACOB   Your employer. He seems a bit... affected.

JOSEPH   You could say that, yes. *(pause)* He has a certain... distance. It's his style.

They smile at each other.

JACOB   How'd you do it?

JOSEPH   It's of no consequence.

JACOB   I see.

> *Pause. JACOB sits.*

Please. Sit with me.

> *Pause. JOSEPH sits.*

JACOB   When I was young, I could never talk to my father.
My own fault. I lived in my father's home, always
fighting with my brother. I was the hard shell of a
person, impenetrable. I had to be cut open one day
for the real words to flow. Literally. *(pause)* I left
my father's home, for good. I spent a few days
out on the streets. Searching for myself. One night,
I was drunk, sleeping in an ally. I had a dream.
In my dream, I was climbing a ladder. At the top,
I saw myself as a rich man with a large family,
laughing. All of us together. I tried to speak to this
vision of myself, but I couldn't. My mouth was
filled with blood. So I climbed down the ladder.
And as I descended, I saw myself slowly losing
everything. At the bottom, I saw myself as a poor
man, living alone in squalor. Again, I tried to
speak, but again, my mouth was filled with blood.
I woke up, gagging, and thought, "Oh my God,
this is me. Here I am. Jacob." Nothing to say. No
answer in me. All I can do in this world is give my
own blood. *(pause)* It's an awesome revelation: that
you are, and always will be, in debt.

> *JACOB smiles. He holds up the box.*

This is not a gift for Farrow.

> *JACOB opens the box and takes out the knife.*

Perhaps your children will find a use for it,
someday.

*JACOB hands JOSEPH the knife. JOSEPH takes it.
JACOB stands.*

You're a busy man. I'll be going.

JOSEPH stands.

JOSEPH   Oh. I...

*Pause. They look at each other. JOSEPH holds out
his hand.*

My employer and I congratulate you. We wish you
the best of luck.

*They shake hands. Pause. They come together and
hug each other.*

JACOB   Now I can die.

The end.

THE KABBALISTIC
PSYCHOANALYSIS OF
ADAM R. TZADDIK

The Kabbalistic Psychoanalysis of Adam R. Tzaddik was first produced at SummerWorks, Toronto, August, 1998, with the following cast:

Doctor   Terrence Bryant
Adam   Graeme Somerville

Directed by Chris Abraham
Stage Managed by Stephen Finney

Other productions were important to the development of the play and include:

Ashkenaz Festival, Toronto, September, 1999.
MAI Theatre, Montreal, November, 1999.

Doctor   Terrence Bryant
Adam   Paul Fauteux
Directed by Chris Abraham

Produced by Moriah Productions and Theatre Passe Muraille, Toronto, November, 2000.

Doctor   Terrence Bryant
Adam   Paul Fauteux
Directed by Chris Abraham
Stage Managed by Beth Brown
Lighting Design by Steve Lucas

CHARACTERS

ADAM
DOCTOR

PRELUDE: EIN-SOF

ADAM   So this is psychoanalysis?

DOCTOR   Not yet, no. The beginning, perhaps.

ADAM   The beginning, right. Do you believe in God?

DOCTOR   Why do you ask?

ADAM   I'm curious. Do you believe in God? *(pause)* You're not answering the question.

DOCTOR   No. I'm not. It's.... *(pause)* I think you'll find it more useful for us to talk about why you ask certain questions than for us to talk about the answers.

ADAM   I see.

            Pause.

DOCTOR   Do I believe in God...

ADAM   I want to know if it's true.

DOCTOR   If what's true?

ADAM   That psychoanalysts are atheists. *(pause)* I believe in God.

DOCTOR   So does it matter what I believe?

ADAM   I need your help.

DOCTOR   With what?

ADAM   With my release. My obliteration.

DOCTOR   Obliteration? *(pause)* I take it you're unhappy.

ADAM   No, not really.

DOCTOR   You're not?

ADAM   No.

DOCTOR   Are you sure?

ADAM   Yes. I'm just turbulent. That's it.

DOCTOR   I see. So then why... I mean, this isn't just... did something happen? Has something been bothering you?

ADAM   I've barely left the walls of my apartment in four years.

DOCTOR   Okay.

ADAM   I get all my food delivered.

DOCTOR   Yes.

ADAM   All I do is sit, alone, and sometimes read.

DOCTOR   Good.

ADAM   What's good?

DOCTOR   Not good. Better. *(pause)* This is better.

ADAM   Better to talk about?

DOCTOR   Yes.

ADAM   You mean the way it sounds?

DOCTOR   It sounds like a problem. To sit alone for four years. And you're here to talk about it.

ADAM   The earmarks of a problem. *(pause)* Nothing's been bothering me. Not as you mean. It's much deeper than that.

DOCTOR   Oh?

ADAM   I'm trying to get to the essence. That's why I'm here. To go beneath the surface of illusions. Down to the deep sea, below the turmoil of waves.

DOCTOR   You're turbulent, now.

ADAM   Yes.

DOCTOR   And you want to get beneath.

ADAM   That's right.

DOCTOR   Tell me. What, exactly, is the essence? Where is it you're going?

> *ADAM smiles.*

ADAM   It's useless to talk about it. The essence is that without end. It can be referred to, but never really touched.

DOCTOR   So we're in a bit of trouble, then. *(pause)* Surely, there's some way to speak of it. Some way of putting it into words.

ADAM   There is a book...

DOCTOR   Yes?

ADAM   Called the *Zohar*.

DOCTOR   The *Zohar*.

ADAM   But I'd rather not talk about it.

DOCTOR   Why not?

ADAM   It's a forbidden, sacred and mysterious text.

DOCTOR   Eureka.

> *Pause.*

ADAM   So I need to talk about it.

DOCTOR   I think so, yes. It's the only way we can proceed.

ADAM   The *Zohar*'s a religious text. Ancient and poetic.
A Jewish text. About the formation of God. It's a
genuine myth of divine self-creation. The *Zohar*
describes how the essence of God is nothing.
Literally, nothing. No light, no texture, no desire.
God is created from this absence. Can you imagine?

DOCTOR   No.

ADAM   Nothing. As an essence.

DOCTOR   Of course, there is–

ADAM   What?

DOCTOR   Something.

ADAM   Where?

DOCTOR   Underneath. Where you're going.

ADAM   No. See, that's the thing. Nothingness is the most
hidden. The most underneath. The substance of God,
His ten manifestations, they are layers on top.
Superstructure, after thoughts. I am certain of this.
I have spent years–

DOCTOR   Sitting. Alone.

ADAM   Look, I shouldn't talk about this.

DOCTOR   What better place to talk about the forbidden than in
the office of a psychoanalyst? *(pause)* You are in the
rough turbulence of waves. Drifting on the surface
of a great sea. And you long for the peace that's
underneath. The peace of nothingness, like the quiet
of the sea's centre. I don't blame you. Nothingness
is an intoxicating promise. But the turbulence runs
deeper than you imagine, I think. The waves are
mere symptoms of a very real, articulate pain at the
core. So to claim there's nothing, that's an easier
position to take.

ADAM   It is?

DOCTOR   Yes.

ADAM   Oh. *(pause)* I disagree with you.

DOCTOR   I know. Give it time. What's really underneath, we'll have to see.

ADAM   My family?

DOCTOR   Very possibly.

ADAM   Probably?

DOCTOR   Yes, probably.

ADAM   The *Zohar* speaks of God's manifestations. Sefiroth, they're called. Some of them are characterized by familial categories. There's Hokhmah, the father in God. Binah, the mother. Tif'eret, the son or divine Self in God. And Shekhinah, the sister and bride in God.

DOCTOR   The sister and bride?

ADAM   Yes.

DOCTOR   Both?

ADAM   Yes, both. Amazing that it could be both.

> *ADAM fidgets.*

DOCTOR   This upsets you.

ADAM   No.

DOCTOR   You're shifting.

ADAM   It's nothing, really. A few bumps and etches on my otherwise clean slate. *(pause)* A few deep breaths. Let 'em fade away.

DOCTOR   Do you have a sister?

ADAM   Yeah, I do.

DOCTOR   Good.

ADAM   My sister is good?

DOCTOR   Just continue talking.

            Pause.

ADAM   The problem is I want to call my sister. I feel the urge
            to call her. And others, too. Friends, ex-lovers. Which
            means reaching outside. I have this urge, in spite of
            my knowledge.

DOCTOR   What knowledge?

ADAM   The essence of the *Zohar*. The non-essence of God.

DOCTOR   The mythical quiet you imagine at the core?

ADAM   It's not myth. There are mystics who sit alone, in
            silence, for hours at a time. Doing nothing. Just sit-
            ting, losing themselves in their own breathing. They
            cease to want. They lose all desire. These are holy
            people. They exist in every religion, in every belief
            system.

DOCTOR   I've read about them.

ADAM   Yes.

DOCTOR   But they, too, are human beings. With normal urges
            and desires. Adam, you don't have to renounce your-
            self. You should have the freedom to desire. To expe-
            rience the world. The freedom to call your sister.

ADAM   They sit alone, in silence, and let the flourishes float
            away.

DOCTOR   May I ask you something? *(pause)* Are you suffering?

ADAM   It doesn't matter. I don't really care if I'm suffering or
            not.

SCENE ONE: KETER

ADAM   Free association?

DOCTOR   That's right.

ADAM   Begin talking and just go with the flow.

DOCTOR   You can start with cabbages and go until you've moved to kings. That's the way Sigmund Freud described it.

ADAM   Cabbages to kings. *(pause)* A genius idea, free association. So creative.

DOCTOR   Why don't you give it a try?

ADAM   Cabbages are lettuce-like. "Let us" begin.

> *ADAM smiles.*

Puns are good, aren't they?

DOCTOR   Sometimes.

ADAM   Beginnings. In Russia, at the beginning of the twentieth century, realism was all the rage. Rage... there's an emotion I feel rarely. What else is rare? Now that the human population has exploded, one-time plentiful animals have become rare. We kill them, the animals. Then eat them. Roasted or fried or baked. Judaism has dietary laws, Kosher laws. They restrict the number of edible animals to only a few specific ones. What makes an animal specific? Fur and eyes, teeth and muscle. These are external flourishes. The final, finishing touches. The scary parts of animals. Also, the things we love about them.

DOCTOR   Go on.

ADAM   This is nothing.

DOCTOR   You were saying... about animals...

ADAM   Just a thought. Animals are superfluous. *(pause)*
I don't have anything else to say.

DOCTOR You don't want to talk about anything that might
lead you to the pain.

ADAM   There is no pain.

DOCTOR Oh?

ADAM   I mean, my pain is superficial. The pain is not my
core.

DOCTOR Right. There is nothingness at the core. So you say.
But I say that nothingness is, in fact, a pure, blinding
pain. And this pain can cause words to come forth.
In free association. And then your words will reflect
back on the untouchable, insurmountable pain at the
origin, spurring it further into words, finally giving it
some form, some format, some expression. *(pause)*
Talk about whatever you like. Find a productive
topic.

ADAM   What's a productive topic?

DOCTOR You'll know when you feel it.

ADAM   Feel what?

DOCTOR The effects of your speaking. The birth of something
real from a mere flow of words.

        ADAM smiles.

This reminds you of something? What I'm saying.

ADAM   The *Zohar*.

DOCTOR Your sacred Jewish text?

ADAM   There are ten sefiroth, ten manifestations of God.
The first is called Keter, the crown. Its purpose is to
de-lineate the boundaries of God. To put the first
borders on nothingness. Keter is the nebulous zone

> where Godly thought begins. It is divine thought in
> its purest state.

DOCTOR   Like free association?

ADAM   Well, that's what I was...

DOCTOR   Yes.

ADAM   I was thinking.

DOCTOR   The borders of nothingness.

> *Pause.*

ADAM   You're annoyed.

DOCTOR   Is that what you imagine?

ADAM   No. You are.

DOCTOR   I'm not annoyed.

ADAM   You don't think the *Zohar* is a productive topic.

DOCTOR   We're not building a fence around nothingness. This
is not about God, it's about your concrete self.

ADAM   Right.

DOCTOR   You have thoughts, like you said, the fear and love of
an animal's characteristics.

ADAM   Thoughts float in and out, here, then away.

DOCTOR   They have weight...

ADAM   They're cleared and abandoned with a few simple
breaths.

DOCTOR   ...they must be given weight.

ADAM   Why?

Pause.

DOCTOR   Why do you think?

Pause.

ADAM   I have a question. If Keter is the free association of a non-existent God, then who is doing the free associating?

DOCTOR   Adam...

ADAM   How can pre-divine free association really be a possibility? I mean, the drifting thoughts of a God that doesn't yet exist?

The DOCTOR sighs.

That makes no sense to me.

DOCTOR   We're not talking about God. We're talking about you.

ADAM   We are God's creatures. Made in God's image. With the same essence at our core.

DOCTOR   You know, I often see patients use religious issues to cover-up more personal ones.

ADAM   That's just testament to their lack of profound religious thought.

The DOCTOR laughs.

DOCTOR   Fair enough. *(pause)* Look, Adam. We're not capable of uncovering God's essence. This is a doctor's office, not a holy place. If you bring up religious issues, that's fine. But my job is to point out the ways in which those religious issues might cover-up or displace personal ones. We are here to learn about your mind. And your mind is a measurable, testable, treatable document. *(pause)* Which is not to say your religious questions or beliefs have no value. They're just not productive here.

ADAM I feel snared and barbed by a hook and a net.

DOCTOR You have to just go with the flow. Free associate, not philosophize.

ADAM Go with the flow. I understand.

DOCTOR You're afraid.

ADAM Go with the flow. No fighting the waves. Breathe... breathe and let go.

SCENE TWO: HOKHMAH

ADAM Apple. Apple, apple, apple. Apple reminds me of seeds. Seeds remind me of semen. Semen reminds me of pornography. Pornography reminds me of horses. Horses remind me of jousting. Jousting reminds me of kings. Kings remind me of cabbage. Cabbage reminds me of borscht. Borscht reminds me of Poland. Poland reminds me of pogroms. Pogroms remind me of Nazis. Nazis remind me of Anne Frank. Anne Frank reminds me of Amsterdam. Amsterdam reminds me of hashish. Hashish reminds me of pipes. Pipes remind me of lip and tongue cancer. Lip and tongue cancer reminds me of Sigmund Freud. Sigmund Freud reminds me of you. You remind me of a quadriplegic. Quadriplegics remind me of wheelchairs. Wheelchairs remind me of access ramps. Access ramps remind me of ski lifts. Ski lifts remind me of mid-mountain chalets. Mid-mountain chalets remind me of hot cinnamon cider. Hot cinnamon cider reminds me of apples. Hey, I returned to apples.

DOCTOR Do apples make you think of anything?

ADAM They seem to make me think of themselves.

DOCTOR Go on.

ADAM Apples. *(pause)* Nothing. A circle beginning and ending with an apple. There's the picture of one in my head. Red. The perfect apple shape. Little leaf sticking off the stem.

DOCTOR   Do you picture it alone in your mind? Or is there a scene? Does it remind you of anything in particular?

ADAM   No, only itself. The image of an apple. Contained.

DOCTOR   Right.

ADAM   Ap-ple. Ap-ple.

DOCTOR   What are you saying?

ADAM   I'm thinking about the word.

DOCTOR   A pull.

ADAM   Excuse me?

DOCTOR   The way you said it. Sounded like "a pull".

ADAM   A pull...

DOCTOR   Perhaps something pulling on your mind. Pulling you into your apartment and keeping you there. Preventing any further thought, any escape. Almost like gravity.

ADAM   I made a Freudian slip, you mean.

DOCTOR   Double meanings are a way in which vital information from your unconscious mind is hidden in what you say.

ADAM   Yeah...

DOCTOR   It's a point of entry for us. This apple can be like a seed for your thoughts. From it, almost anything we need to know about your unconscious mind can grow.

ADAM   But the apple, it's...

DOCTOR   What?

ADAM   ...just an image. I mean, a word, a thought. Part of the flow.

DOCTOR   The apple is a pull. You said it yourself.

ADAM   Okay, but...

DOCTOR   I know it's difficult to accept. That your mind could work in this way.

ADAM   ...this interrupts the flow. Go with the flow, you said.

DOCTOR   Until you hit a point.

ADAM   But I could have stopped anywhere. Anne Frank, or mid-mountain chalets.

DOCTOR   It's real, Adam. A fixed point and a pull.

ADAM   Oh. A manifestation. A first point. That's what you mean.

DOCTOR   This makes sense to you?

ADAM   Now it does. Yes.

DOCTOR   Why suddenly?

ADAM   Hokhmah.

DOCTOR   Excuse me?

ADAM   It's just like you said. A point that emerges from the flow.

DOCTOR   From the *Zohar*?

ADAM   This should be a discovery, not a conversation.

DOCTOR   It is a discovery. I'm trying to discover you.

ADAM   The mystics describe Hokhmah as a single,
            concentrated point, too small to see. It's like a
            sperm, or a seed, that's somehow created during the
            pre-divine free association, Keter. From this point, all
            of God's Being grows. Hokhmah's like the father of
            God's mind. Like the apple. All is contained within.

DOCTOR   But that's mythological.

ADAM   So are we.

DOCTOR   You are flesh and blood. You have a mind. *(pause)*
            You're turbulent. Like you said. Snared and hooked
            in a net.

ADAM   That I am.

DOCTOR   Caught by a great big "pull". Correct?

ADAM   A superficial pull. The pull of illusory thoughts and
            images. There's nothing real here.

DOCTOR   I think there's something very real.

ADAM   You mean the apple has substance. It's the origin of
            something, the sperm or seed of my unconscious
            mind. It's the point Hokhmah, appearing amidst the
            free association of Keter. And all of this is part of a
            very real process. The mythological unfolding of
            myself. Is that what you mean?

DOCTOR   Mmm...

ADAM   What?

DOCTOR   This is... these are not the right terms.

ADAM   They aren't?

DOCTOR   We need to find something different. Some kind of
            different approach.

ADAM   No more talk of the *Zohar*?

DOCTOR   Not necessarily. It's just... there are some basics here, Adam. Some things you'll have to accept. Your mind is driving this process. And your thoughts have meaning. When you say apple, you may really mean "a pull".

ADAM   Sometimes an apple is just an apple.

DOCTOR   But if it's more... if it's "a pull"...

ADAM   Yeah?

DOCTOR   Then we've begun.

SCENE THREE: BINAH

ADAM   Around the apple, what do I see? I see trees and bees and fields. And inside the apple I see seeds and worms and juice. Now I'm taking my apple and I'm putting it on a tree. A tree, an apple tree. Okay, I can see it. I see a field around the tree. Long field grass and other trees nearby. It's a scene, I can see the scene. I know what it is. My father, when we were kids, he took us to this field behind our house in autumn and we'd pick apples. He loved it, my dad. Get so excited. My sister and I, we'd climb the trees and pick fruit. From below us, on the ground, our father would shout up encouragement. Various forms of praise. So we'd smile down at him.

DOCTOR   Your sister and you.

ADAM   Yeah. And sometimes my mother would come with us. Usually, she'd sit out in the field grass in the distance, just watch us pick fruit. I'd glance over, see her watching. She surveyed this scene as if it were hers to control. I always wondered what she thought of us.

    Long pause.

DOCTOR   Go on.

ADAM   What did she think of us?

DOCTOR   What do you imagine?

ADAM   I don't know. It's all hazy to me, now. *(pause)* The unfolding of the apple.

DOCTOR   Yes.

ADAM   What do you think?

DOCTOR   I think if you continue to free associate on the scene you've provided, we'll begin to discover some valuable information about your unconscious mind.

ADAM   You mean stuff. Material stuff. My family.

DOCTOR   We'll have to wait and see.

ADAM   Conflicts or problems. Something psychologically real.

DOCTOR   I think talking about the scene's function prevents us from further discussing the scene itself.

ADAM   And from giving it any weight.

DOCTOR   Tell me more.

ADAM   I can picture everyone there. My mother, my father, my sister and myself. It's everything, all at once.

DOCTOR   What everything?

ADAM   All points all at once. There's the apple, which is Hokhmah, the concentrated point. And now we've uncovered Binah, which is the scene surrounding it. Unfolding around the apple.

DOCTOR   Sounds like the *Zohar*.

ADAM   Yeah.

DOCTOR   Tell me about it.

ADAM   No, it doesn't matter.

DOCTOR   It doesn't?

ADAM   No. It's just a flourish.

DOCTOR   What is Binah? You said it's the scene surrounding the apple, Hokhmah. What does that mean?

ADAM   Binah's called the mother in God. Or the womb of God. Just as Hokhmah is a concentrated point, so Binah is the distribution of all points, all at once. Binah is infinitely huge, while Hokhmah is infinitely small. They're related to each other. The God that humans know, God the divine Self, is created when you plant the seed Hokhmah into the womb Binah. Within that womb, the seed grows.

DOCTOR   So it's the birth of something. Or at least the point of conception.

ADAM   Not just something. It's the conception of God.

DOCTOR   How does this relate to the apple and scene in your mind?

ADAM   It just makes sense. They remind me of each other. Within my scene is the divine point, the apple. But now there's a surrounding scenario which contains all points, all at once, like Binah the womb. Hokhmah, the apple, is growing within that scene. *(pause)* But all of that's a cover for the essence of calm, pure nothing flowing through it all. *(pause)* I mean, it has to be. Doesn't it?

    Pause.

DOCTOR   Still, you're not talking about your family. You've brought up a scene with concrete references to your family, and yet you're not talking about them. *(pause)* You are avoiding the substance of your associations.

ADAM   But my family... they're only manifestations. Illusions and flourishes that cover the nothingness within.

DOCTOR   Right. *(pause)* You know, I'm very curious...

ADAM   What?

DOCTOR   I'm not at all sure...

ADAM   Of?

DOCTOR   ...of what you're doing. Why are you here?

ADAM   I'm here for my problems. To see what they are so I can sweep them away.

DOCTOR   This all fits together for you. The *Zohar* and analysis. Like a big, divine conspiracy.

ADAM   I know...

DOCTOR   Why?

ADAM   I... I don't know. I've never thought about anything like this before.

DOCTOR   It's almost like a test...

ADAM   I'm just doing this, like you said. Following the flow.

DOCTOR   A religious test of psychoanalysis.

ADAM   I am not testing you. *(pause)* This is my life, doctor. My mind. It has nothing to do with you.

SCENE FOUR: HESED

ADAM   I must look like a fool to you.

DOCTOR   Why do you say that?

ADAM   You think I'm a religious freak.

DOCTOR   I have no opinion about your religious belief.

ADAM   I don't believe you.

DOCTOR   Why not?

ADAM   You disagree with God. I mean, the essence of God.

DOCTOR   And that upsets you.

ADAM   Right.

DOCTOR   Because...

ADAM   You have scorn for me. You must to disagree.

       Pause.

DOCTOR   Adam, I hope you'll forgive me. Please understand, I don't scorn you for anything you believe, do, think or say.

ADAM   I'm not as religious as you might think. I don't leave my apartment to go to synagogue. I don't read the standard religious books, really. Like the Talmud or the Shulhan Aruch. I don't say prayers in the morning, put on a tallit, or wear a kippah. Any genuinely observant Jew would look at me and consider me an assimilated atheist. *(pause)* If anything, I'm more like you than them.

       Pause.

DOCTOR   Tell me something more about your family.

ADAM   Okay. *(pause)* My father. He's a man who smiles frequently. He's kind to his core. When I picture him in my mind, I'm looking at him from above. Me, looking down on him. From my place in the trees, picking apples. My father whistles when he picks apples. When I come down from my tree limbs, even if I've practically no apples in my basket, my father always, without fail, tells me what a good job I've done. How well I did up in the trees. *(pause)*

He listens to me. Always. He is so kind. *(pause)*
I could be in the trees cursing him, but when I come
down he praises me for my effort.

DOCTOR   When was the last time you saw your father?

ADAM   I don't know. Years. I'm afraid to go down and see
him.

DOCTOR   Go down?

ADAM   Down to where he lives.

DOCTOR   From where you live, holed up in the apple tree.

ADAM   Even when I was a misbehaving, snivelling brat my
father would give me the best apple from his bushel
to snack on while we worked.

DOCTOR   Nice father.

ADAM   Yes.

DOCTOR   Always willing to forgive.

ADAM   That's right. *(pause)* You're good at what you do.

DOCTOR   Oh? Why?

ADAM   You always listen. You always encourage me, even
when I'm undeserving.

DOCTOR   Why would you be undeserving? *(pause)* Hello?

ADAM   I don't know why.

    Pause.

DOCTOR   Let's get back to your father.

ADAM   He's always willing to forgive.

    Pause.

DOCTOR Go on.

ADAM A merciful man.

DOCTOR Yes.

ADAM Merciful, like you.

DOCTOR Like me?

ADAM Of course. Both of you. Like each other and...

DOCTOR Do you see what you're doing?

ADAM ...and like Hesed.

DOCTOR You are playing to me as if I were your father.

ADAM The next unfolding. The mercy of the father.

DOCTOR Because you want me to forgive you...

ADAM The fourth manifestation.

DOCTOR ...just like you want your father to forgive you.

ADAM It makes perfect sense.

DOCTOR But forgive you for what?

ADAM It makes such perfect sense.

DOCTOR Did you hear what I said?

ADAM Yes. I am playing to you as I would to my father. Because I want my father's mercy. So I treat you as him, in a relationship of transference.

DOCTOR That's right. *(pause)* And you were saying? Something about the next unfolding.

ADAM Yes. Hesed. It's the first concrete aspect of the divine. Born from the womb Binah and the seed Hokhmah. Hesed is an attribute of the father in

God. An attribute that both you and my father share. *(pause)* Hesed is mercy.

DOCTOR   Mercy for what?

ADAM   For the world. For everything that will soon follow.

DOCTOR   I don't mean God, I mean your father. He has mercy. For what?

ADAM   That doesn't matter.

DOCTOR   Of course it does. The *Zohar*... means nothing more than what it means to you.

ADAM   Right.

DOCTOR   Good.

ADAM   I'm sorry.

> *Pause.*

DOCTOR   No, I apologize.

ADAM   I'm wasting your time.

DOCTOR   No. No, I just.... *(pause)* This is.... You have an incredible defense.

ADAM   I feel terrible. I'm sorry.

DOCTOR   I'm not the type of person who usually looks to religious texts to find the meaning of a personal neurosis.

ADAM   I don't have a neurosis.

DOCTOR   Nor am I a very big fan of Carl Jung.

ADAM   You're putting too much weight on my feelings. They don't mean anything.

DOCTOR   You've just experienced transference. That only comes from unconscious desire.

ADAM   That doesn't mean it's deep or real or important. It's just the flourish of desire.

DOCTOR   Why are you so afraid to have your desires mean anything?

ADAM   Because that makes God petty. And it makes me a brute and a bore.

DOCTOR   What you're doing here has been very normal. Transference. You, slipping into the part of a child who wants forgiveness, with me in the role of your father. Like every other patient.

ADAM   Yes.

DOCTOR   Does that have no power for you? Doesn't that convince you of a self that's somewhere underneath? Somewhere hard at work?

ADAM   It just means there's still more work to wipe myself away.

          Pause.

DOCTOR   Adam, this is you we're talking about. Not God and not the *Zohar*. Something that comes from you and only reflects back on yourself.

ADAM   I know.

          ADAM shifts.

DOCTOR   What's wrong?

ADAM   Nothing's wrong. Nothing.

SCENE FIVE: DIN

DOCTOR   I don't think we can continue like this.

ADAM   What?

DOCTOR   We need to change our tactics.

ADAM   You don't like me, do you?

DOCTOR   No. No, that's not it at all...

ADAM   You think my beliefs are delusions and my presence is a test.

DOCTOR   No.

ADAM   Have the guts to just say it.

DOCTOR   We're confusing issues and grinding our gears...

ADAM   Stop denying the truth.

DOCTOR   Hatred of you is not the truth.

ADAM   But I can feel it. Your judgment.

DOCTOR   Just because you feel it doesn't mean it comes from me.

ADAM   Where else could it come from?

DOCTOR   From yourself.

>   *ADAM laughs.*

>   Adam, I am not judging you.

ADAM   You're a liar.

DOCTOR   Oh?

ADAM   That's all there is to say about it.

DOCTOR   Try to say more.

ADAM   No. I'm done.

DOCTOR   I think this could be productive territory.

ADAM   I thought we couldn't continue like this. *(pause)* You know, you're supposed to be impartial. With no judgment for me, whatsoever. No anything. Just a placid, objective shell who watches and listens. That's what I want from you. That's why I'm here.

DOCTOR   Where are you?

ADAM   What?

DOCTOR   Describe to me where you are.

ADAM   Where...?

DOCTOR   No hesitation, just describe.

ADAM   I'm here, alone, in your office...

DOCTOR   Faster.

ADAM   ...on display. On the couch, in front of you, in your line of sight, your line of fire, you can see what I'm doing and you hate it, hate me, who I am. You can see my thoughts and you're convinced they matter, which they don't. You've seen me, seen it, and you hate me. I'm in your perfect sight.

DOCTOR   High or low?

ADAM   High. *(pause)* What...

DOCTOR   And where am I?

ADAM   Out away from me. Distant. In the fields. *(pause)* Oh God.

DOCTOR   You see?

ADAM   Yeah.

DOCTOR   Tell me.

ADAM   Transference, again.

DOCTOR   That's right.

ADAM   But now you're my mother. Judging me out in the fields. While I'm here, up high, in the apple tree.

DOCTOR   That's correct. And it came from you. From the workings of your own mind. It has nothing to do with me. *(pause)* You are in need of psychoanalysis. You have a self that's in pain, underneath.

ADAM   I'm finished coming here.

DOCTOR   It hurts you too much.

ADAM   No.

DOCTOR   You're so afraid the "flourishes" are real.

ADAM   You keep insisting on something that I don't believe.

DOCTOR   And you keep discussing an ancient Jewish text which I have no choice but to believe. *(pause)* So we're hurting together, then.

ADAM   You're not hurting.

DOCTOR   We both are. You feel judged by me. Although, in truth, it's you judging yourself. And I... I have understood you incorrectly. With a... skepticism that perhaps has overstepped its bounds. That is both embarrassing and painful to me.

ADAM   Products of judgment. Our pain.

DOCTOR   So it seems.

ADAM   It makes sense we'd feel that.

DOCTOR   It certainly does.

> *Pause. ADAM smiles.*

The *Zohar*, again?

ADAM   Yes. You're guiding the flow. I can't help but think of it.

DOCTOR   You know, your *Zohar*, it makes sense to me.

ADAM   I don't want to cause any more trouble.

DOCTOR   Your religious mythology makes perfect scientific sense. *(pause)* The *Zohar*, you were saying...

ADAM   I don't want to keep talking about it. It's just more empty manifestations.

DOCTOR   We were talking about judgment. The pain we both feel. The pain of judgment. Can you clarify that for me?

ADAM   Din means judgment.

DOCTOR   Of course it does.

ADAM   Din is an attribute of the mother in God.

DOCTOR   So, it's like your mother's imagined judgment. Like the transference you just experienced.

ADAM   Din is the counter-balance to the mercy of Hesed. You see, Hesed alone, pure mercy, is too all-powerful. Nothing can move forward or be created in its blissful white wash. For God to become fully Himself, the great limiting power of Din must curb the all pervasive power of Hesed. This allows for balance and development. Din is a judgment that's strict and hard, but good. It causes pain sometimes, but it's necessary.

DOCTOR   Is it really?

ADAM God cannot become himself without the balancing power of Din.

DOCTOR And so neither can you?

SCENE SIX: TIF'ERET

DOCTOR How are you feeling?

ADAM I oscillate.

DOCTOR Between what and what?

ADAM Between the desire for your mercy and the fear of your judgment.

DOCTOR Between the two transferences.

ADAM Yes. *(pause)* I should just talk.

DOCTOR Yes, I think that's a good idea.

ADAM I'll try. *(pause)* I can't really speak in a way I feel comfortable. Suddenly, I'm afraid everything I say is some kind of appeal to you. Either for your mercy, or just an attempt to mitigate your judgments. What I imagine are judgments. Why should I make those appeals? I shouldn't need or want anything at all. I shouldn't want your mercy and I shouldn't mind your judgment. *(pause)* Release. Please, release. Breathe and let go.

DOCTOR You do want something. Mercy and forgiveness for something unspoken.

ADAM I don't want to want.

DOCTOR But you do. It's a fact. It's why you're here.

ADAM That's not why I'm here! I'm here so I can return to my core of nothingness.

DOCTOR   Adam, when the *Zohar* was written people didn't
          have psychoanalysis. Back then, the best way of
          getting inside of the self was to look outside, to God.
          There, in the heavens, the author of your awesome
          book imagined he saw the mirror image of himself.
          His own personal traumas and needs, he projected
          onto God. The so-called flourishes of desire we've
          been discussing are, in fact, part of an ancient
          psychoanalysis. That of the author.

ADAM   I am not the author.

DOCTOR   In here, you're the transmitter of his text. And so yes,
          that makes you, temporarily, the author of the *Zohar*.

ADAM   No...

DOCTOR   Yes. I'm neither your mother nor your father. They're
          not here in this room. But they are present in your
          mind. You project them onto me. Your mother's
          judgment and your father's mercy, you possess
          them both. That's what makes you a person. So use
          them as you wish. Be kind and stern with yourself
          as you need. Remember, you're in control here.
          You're our only concern. You're Adam R. Tzaddik,
          an individual, our subject. Do you understand? Your
          mother, your father, your sister, they're only here as
          they're filtered through you.

ADAM   Of course.

DOCTOR   Adam R. Tzaddik, he's the entire world in this office.
          Without you, our work is nothing.

ADAM   It all has to do with me.

DOCTOR   It's your psychoanalysis.

ADAM   I understand. *(pause)* Have you been studying the
          Zohar?

DOCTOR   Not really, no.

ADAM   You don't realize what you just said?

DOCTOR   What do you mean?

ADAM   About Tif'eret.

DOCTOR   No. Tif'eret?

ADAM   What you just said to me.

DOCTOR   What I say is true for all my patients.

ADAM   So it's something universal to psychoanalysis?

DOCTOR   The patient is never wrong. What he or she feels is everything. In every case.

ADAM   But that's Tif'eret. Tif'eret's just like the patient. I mean, in analogy. The master. The world's representative. *(pause)* Tif'eret is the balance of Hesed and Din. The balance of judgment and mercy, inside the divine Self, the body of God. Tif'eret is the one true name of God. The "yud, hay, vuv, hay" written in the Torah. God as He appears in the world, God to whom human prayers are directed, God that spoke to Moses from Sinai, on the mountain top.

   The DOCTOR laughs.

ADAM   Why are you laughing?

DOCTOR   I just can't win with you, can I?

ADAM   Win what?

DOCTOR   Well, Adam, congratulations. I really don't think I can help you much more.

ADAM   What does that mean?

DOCTOR   You know, I've never.... You have me stumped.

ADAM   Stumped?

DOCTOR   I can't... I...

ADAM   Are you quitting?

DOCTOR   There's always some reference to the divine. Always
            some double meaning drawing our process outside
            of yourself and into something mystical.

ADAM   You can't give up. I refuse to let you.

DOCTOR   Oh?

ADAM   We have more to do. There's all that transference.
            My mother, my dad, the apple and tree and that
            whole scene.

DOCTOR   Empty flourishes.

ADAM   Well, I'm not done with them, yet. I don't feel them
            wiped away. *(pause)* I want the notes.

DOCTOR   What?

ADAM   The notes from our sessions. Give them to me.

DOCTOR   They're not yours. You can't have them.

ADAM   I insist.

DOCTOR   Who are you to insist?

ADAM   I'm, I'm the patient!

DOCTOR   So what?

ADAM   Look, they're words about me, Adam R. Tzaddik,
            your patient. About what I said in here, what I feel
            and packed into an envelope with my name on the
            outside, and that makes them mine, okay? And
            I want them back. They're mine. *(pause)* Mine!

SCENE SEVEN: NETZAH

DOCTOR   I want you to tell me what's next. *(pause)* The *Zohar*. What's next?

ADAM   So you want to continue?

DOCTOR   The next sefirah. After Tif'eret.

ADAM   Netzah.

DOCTOR   Tell me about it.

ADAM   It's called God's triumph.

DOCTOR   Go on.

ADAM   Netzah is an attribute of Tif'eret. It's one of God's tools. It's God's mercy. It comes from pure mercy, from Hesed, but Netzah is a more diluted version. It's more practical. Mercy as applied to real situations. To specific people, or specific events.

DOCTOR   So it's a personal characteristic of an already formed God.

ADAM   Yeah. A tool the divine Self can use on the universe.

DOCTOR   I understand. *(pause)* Hello?

    Long pause.

    Adam? Are you there?

    ADAM starts crying.

    Why are you crying?

ADAM   I don't know... I...

DOCTOR   Are you okay?

ADAM   I don't know.

> *Pause. ADAM continues to cry.*

ADAM   I have to leave. I can't talk to you anymore.

DOCTOR   Who are you talking to?

ADAM   God, I'm going to miss you.

DOCTOR   Who are you saying that to. Not me.

ADAM   My father.

DOCTOR   Yes, your father. You want mercy from your father, you want mercy from me.

ADAM   Yes.

DOCTOR   But what have you done that makes you feel so terrible?

SCENE EIGHT: HOD

ADAM   Oh God... something's wrong. I... don't feel so good. *(pause)* My heart's really... I don't know what, it's really... fast...

> *ADAM checks his pulse.*

I gotta do something. My breathing, I... I can't breathe...

DOCTOR   You're hyperventilating.

ADAM   No, my heart. It's a heart attack... it's what... I can't, I can't help it...

DOCTOR   Calm down.

ADAM   Call a doctor. Please call a doctor. I need a doctor, now, please.

DOCTOR   I am a doctor.

ADAM   I'm having a heart attack!

DOCTOR   No, you're not.

ADAM   Oh God.... Oh God, I'm dying.... Please...

DOCTOR   Relax.

ADAM   Please...

DOCTOR   Take deep breaths.

ADAM   Please.

DOCTOR   A racing heart is a common symptom of panic.

>   *ADAM takes deep breaths.*

>   Good.

ADAM   What's wrong with me? What the fuck is wrong with me?

DOCTOR   You're afraid.

ADAM   You were looking at me.

DOCTOR   That's all I was doing.

ADAM   Stop looking at me!

DOCTOR   Okay.

ADAM   Stop!

DOCTOR   My eyes are closed.

ADAM   I'm sorry. I'm so sorry.

DOCTOR   For what?

>   *Long pause. ADAM calms down a little.*

>   Feel better?

ADAM   I don't know.

DOCTOR   Your heart slowed down?

ADAM   I don't know. *(pause)* I'm not having a heart attack, am I? That was... that was a panic attack.

DOCTOR   A powerful one at that.

ADAM   I can't take this anymore.

DOCTOR   What can't you take?

ADAM   You. Looking at me.

DOCTOR   You imagine that I'm accusing you?

ADAM   Yes.

DOCTOR   Practical judgment. Wracks of torment and pain that you feel in your flesh. Who do you imagine is judging you, Adam? Who sits apart, out in the field, watching you in the apple tree?

ADAM   I know, my mother.

DOCTOR   You want your father's mercy. But it's a mercy you don't believe you deserve. Why not? Because you think you've done something bad, up there in the apple tree. Some kind of sin. And you're afraid that your mother, out in the field, saw you being bad. She is looking at you and judging you. She is looking at you through transference, through me. *(pause)* Hod. Practical judgment. It comes from Din, the pure judgment, but Hod is a more concrete version. Hod is a tool of Tif'eret. The practical tool of judgment used in concrete situations by the divine Self.

ADAM   That's right.

DOCTOR   The judgment within you, our subject. And now, it has turned against you.

    Pause.

ADAM   I'm scared.

DOCTOR   I'll bet.

ADAM   I'm so scared.

DOCTOR   Of what exactly?

ADAM   I don't want to talk about it.

DOCTOR   But you have to.

SCENE NINE: YESOD

DOCTOR   Yesod.

ADAM   The foundation.

DOCTOR   Tell me what you know about it.

ADAM   It's... well... it's God's procreative point. The moment when God reaches into the universe and makes contact with what's outside Him. It's the place from where He creates all material existence.

DOCTOR   Those are euphemisms.

ADAM   They are?

DOCTOR   Yesod. The foundation. The place of power in God. The place where he is active. Here, in this sefirah, is the decision of God. The choice to create.

ADAM   That's right.

DOCTOR   What is it, really?

ADAM   It's God's penis.

DOCTOR   But they never say that. In the *Zohar*.

ADAM   No.

DOCTOR   It's unspoken but it's there.

ADAM   I want to go home.

DOCTOR   Oh?

ADAM   I don't want to continue today.

DOCTOR   Sounds like we're getting somewhere.

ADAM   Can we call it for the day? I don't feel so well.

DOCTOR   Of course we can.

ADAM   Good.

DOCTOR   But then be prepared for more. More years of misery. More years sitting at home, alone. More years lost and stagnate. We are nearing something, here. Don't go home now.

ADAM   I can't do this.

DOCTOR   You are strong and smart. If I can do it, you can do it, too.

ADAM   No. No.

DOCTOR   You know what you've done. It's all laid out in the *Zohar*.

ADAM   No.

DOCTOR   So say it.

ADAM   I don't know what to say.

DOCTOR   Yes, you do.

ADAM   But I can't. I can't just say... I mean, just follow... what does this make me?

DOCTOR   A human being. Like the rest of us.

ADAM What does that make the *Zohar*?

DOCTOR The *Zohar* is a tool. *(pause)* You must decide to speak. You, alone, make the decision. You can always say nothing. Therefore, you alone are the true author of the words. *(pause)* Adam, it will never get more difficult than this. *(pause)* Try. Speak of yourself. Speak of desire and need. Speak about the parts of your existence that you hate and deny. I want to hear you speak about yourself. The real thoughts of Adam R. Tzaddik. *(pause)* You have a choice. Right now, a free choice. Either to go on despite difficulty, or to end this work suddenly, on a whim. That freedom is not just your greatest strength, it's your entire possibility. It's the possibility of righteousness. It is the foundation of all we are doing in this room.

ADAM What have I done?

DOCTOR All the flow has been leading to this. Like a river flowing into the sea. It is inevitable and unavoidable, as painful as that may seem. Still, you have to make the choice to speak.

ADAM The active point. Me. The righteous man.

DOCTOR Tell me about what's next. The Shekhinah. The sister and bride of God.

ADAM It's only me.

DOCTOR Tell me about your sister. We've been waiting for this, you and I. Ever since the beginning. We've come home, at last. Tell me about you and your sister, alone together, united. Unspeakably close. Up above in the apple tree.

SCENE TEN: SHEKHINAH

> *Long pause. ADAM is reading through the DOCTOR's notes on his sessions.*

ADAM So many words about me. *(pause)* It's not like I actually slept with her, is it? *(pause)* And so what if I did? I mean, really? So what? She's not losing any sleep. I wish I had. There. I wish I had. *(pause)* I don't care.

DOCTOR   You don't care.

ADAM   No. Not at all.

>   *He laughs.*

Years of isolated sitting, for what I dreamed and imagined were religious ends. But in truth, nothing sacred. Only fixation and neurosis.

DOCTOR   Ironic, isn't it?

ADAM   It's a sick irony, selfhood. All this looking out and longing to be bigger than what it is.

>   *Pause.*

DOCTOR   You're not as small as you imagine.

ADAM   I'm an insignificant and boring cliché.

DOCTOR   Adam... *(pause)* We're all confined by our particular desires. Every one of us. Your desire lives in the *Zohar*. You long for the Shekhinah. The Shekhinah, such a beautiful concept. Bride of God, sister of God, Sabbath of God, home of God, land of God, feet of God, peace of God, people of God, soul of God, word of God, the very presence of God. You can revel in the Shekhinah. *(pause)* You are a small self, yes, filled with small desires. Eternally small, but that's what allows you to merge with the eternally big. To merge with the Shekhinah. *(pause)* I tell you this, Adam, because you should have enormous pride in your small discoveries. Your neurosis is a great doorway. You feel your trauma so deeply, that it you make it mean the world. *(pause)* Do you understand me?

ADAM   Yes.

DOCTOR   Doesn't that comfort you, a bit?

ADAM   No.

DOCTOR   Why not?

ADAM   A number of years ago, I went to Israel with my
             family. I was sitting in the streets of Safed alone,
             while my parents and sister went to sight-see Isaac
             Luria's synagogue. An old black-hatted Hasid sat
             down next to me and asked me my name. I told him
             Adam R. Tzaddik. His face lit up and he looked at
             me like I was somebody. My son, he scolded, with
             a name like that you've got to move to Israel! The
             initials, see. In Hebrew. Adam begins with Aleph. R
             in Hebrew is the letter Resh. And Tzaddik begins
             with the letter Tzaddie. Aleph, Resh, Tzaddie. Spells
             Eretz. In Hebrew, eretz means land. The land of
             Israel, Eretz, the one true land.

             ADAM laughs.

             You, of all people, my son, your presence belongs in
             Eretz Yisrael! He's all bloated and excited. These
             guys... I tell you... *(pause)* I said... I said, I don't speak
             Hebrew. Aleph, Resh, Tzaddie. Whatever. The
             name's Adam with an "A" and Tzaddik with a "T".
             And if you wanna play name games I'm A-R-T art,
             that's what. *(pause)* I really liked that guy. I mean, he
             was something else. The way he looked at me. Like
             I held the whole future in my hands because of my
             name. Giving a shit about me for no other reason
             than my name. These religious people and their
             words, their deep care for the words... *(pause)* Adam
             R. Tzaddik. I'm here, in this body, this name, and
             I don't speak Hebrew, not very well, and though I've
             tried so hard to reach for God all I've studied is
             myself. This conflict container and jumble of
             Freudian clichés. Pre-civilized thoughts, desire for
             the kin. That's the story of my life. Not the *Zohar*.
             That. It's such small drama, so barely kitchen sink.
             Behold the man, pre-scripted, pre-fabricated! Easy-
             to-assemble mythology man, comes parts complete.
             All packed into this miserable thing. This language,
             this name, this... English, room, couch. Here in these
             things, somewhere Adam, here. In this thing.

DOCTOR You've made a lot of progress...

ADAM My God, what is this? This body, this mythological shell? This breathing, eating, digesting, farting, fucking, bleeding mass of blob? This horrible object? This "I"? What the hell am I?

     The DOCTOR looks at his watch.

DOCTOR I'm sorry but our time is up for now.

     The end.

Anton Piatigorsky studied religion and theatre at Brown University. Three of his plays *The Kabbalistic Psychoanalysis of Adam R. Tzaddik, The Offering* and *Easy Lenny Lazmon and the Great Western Ascension* were nominated for Floyd S. Chalmers Awards, and Dora Mavor Moore outstanding new play awards. *Easy Lenny Lazmon* won four Dora Awards in 1998-1999, including outstanding production and outstanding new play.

ALSO AVAILABLE
BY ANTON PIATIGORSKY

Easy Lenny Lazmon & the Great Western Ascension

Drama

Two exiled travellers head west on an abandoned desert road, searching for the promised land. Encountering a lonely old rancher and his strangely scarred wife, they glimpse the dreams and dangers of their quest. A mystical journey exploring the mythology of western expansion, Jewish history and ancient religious traditions.

First produced in 1998 by Moriah Productions in association with Go Chicken Go at Annex Theatre, Toronto, Ontario.

0-88754-588-2   Year Printed: 2000

2 acts   2m/2f

$13.95

Available from Playwrights Union of Canada
416-703-0201   fax 416-703-0059
orders@puc.ca   http://www.puc.ca